freedom
AT ALL COSTS

A personal journey through the
horrors of war and the raging sea

A TRUE STORY OF TRIAL AND FAITH

DANIEL K. LUC

Freedom At All Costs
by Daniel K. Luc

Printed in the United States of America

ISBN 978-0-615-69666-9

To my mother Kieu Phan Luc
who cares for her children more than herself.

Contents

Foreword

By

Thomas A. ("Drew") Davidson
Major, United States Army (Retired)

On Saturday, August 18, 2001, I received what appeared to be a not-too-rare phone call from what I thought to be a telemarketer. I didn't have "Caller ID" at the time and the following conversation ensued:

Me: "Hello?"

Caller: *(with an indeterminable accent and a remarkable command of English)* "I'm trying to locate a person named Thomas Davidson."

Me: *(expecting some off-the-wall sales pitch, and attempting to not appear too rude)* "I'm Thomas Davidson."

Caller: "I'm looking for a Thomas Davidson who was in the Army."

Me: "I was in the Army. Go on."

Caller: "I'm looking for a Thomas Davidson who was a Major in the Army."

Me: "I was a Major."

Caller: "I'm looking for a Major Thomas Davidson who was with Advisory Team 47 in An Loc, Vietnam in April 1972."

Me: *(now he knows way too much about me and I haven't a clue who he is or where he is going with this)* "So far, you know an awful a lot about me. Just who the h--- are you anyway, and what do you want?"

Caller: "My name is Daniel Luc."

Me: *(getting quite perplexed now)* "I never knew anyone named Daniel Luc."

Caller: "Thieu Ta," *(Vietnamese for 'major')* "I'm Sergeant Tinh, your interpreter."

The (now) unmistakable voice of a person I hadn't heard for over 29 years was on the phone. A person whom I last saw when we simultaneously received military awards from Major General James F. Hollingsworth in Long Binh, Vietnam. A person whom I was certain had been unceremoniously executed at the hands of the communist North Vietnamese when South Vietnam was ultimately overrun. I was certain that Tinh could not possibly have concealed his years of affiliation with the American force in the Republic of Vietnam (RVN).

My mind raced back to a 10-day series of events that began April 4, 1972. Tinh (now "Daniel" Luc) and I shared a sequence of experiences that defies all reason, the survival of which can only be explained as Divine Providence, the protective umbrella of God himself.

The chronological sequences that Daniel Luc has so graphically retold in chapters 6-13 are detailed and quite accurate. Were I to re-tell them, there would be little variation, attributable only to two separate persons' individual perspectives. I'm thrilled that he put it into print. I've tried unsuccessfully for many years.

Acknowledgments

I am not a talented writer, I must admit. It is needless to say I am not talented enough to write a book. As I shared the experiences of my life with many people, common feedback was that I should put my story in writing. Others have even insisted it could be excellent material for a war movie. However, for many years I put that thought aside.

By the end of 2006, the year I turned 60, I decided to take an early retirement from an industrial control business and devote my time to missions work. Now I have more spare time to pursue the dream of writing this book. After more than two years of digging deep into my fading memory, researching the history of the wars in Vietnam and personally interviewing the people involved, this book is finally in your hands. This is the true story of my life. Looking back on the whole sequence of events, the many close calls and incredible encounters can only be explained as God's plan revealed in my life.

I want to express sincere thanks to the many people who have contributed to the completion of this book. The following people deserve special mention:

- John Marrs and Joanne Henninger, dear friends who gave me sound advice on how to write.
- My son Brian who, despite his busy schedule in medical school, helped me find the words to bring this story to life.
- As I tried to be truthful to the story and accurately describe events that took place nearly 40 years ago, I sent a final draft to Thomas

A. Davidson, U.S. Army Major (ret.) with whom I shared my experience during the unthinkable escape from the battle of Loc Ninh, Vietnam. I thank him for providing the foreword to this book, for his attestation to this book's accuracy, and his continued friendship.

- Sharon Nelsen, who was instrumental in helping produce the maps in this book and the final typesetting.
- Pam Nelsen, who added her artistry to this book in designing its beautiful cover.

I also want to thank my dear wife Joyce for her unwavering love and her encouragement in writing this book. For the past thirty-six years she has been by my side — through times of war and times of peace, through good times and bad, and through trials and triumphs. Together we raised two God-fearing children, Irene and Brian. For that, I am truly blessed.

Lastly, I thank my Lord Jesus Christ for his unfailing love. His faithfulness never wavered — even in the darkest hours when it seemed all hope was snuffed out and the world was crumbling around me. He was always there to reassure me: "Son, do not be afraid, for you are mine."

Daniel K. Luc
Fall, 2012

Prologue

It was late on a hot, muggy afternoon in August 1968, the odor of rotting plants permeated the stagnant air. I was an Armed Forces of the Republic of Vietnam (ARVN) sergeant acting as a military interpreter for U.S. Senior District Advisor Capt. Thomas Gallagher. We were accompanying the Chon Thanh District Intelligence Squad on a reconnaissance mission, patrolling the jungle southeast of War Zone C, 45 miles northwest of Saigon. It was only the third day of a five-day operation, but my green jungle fatigues already smelled like a dead rat hanging on my back. The operation had been uneventful. Our only enemy thus far was the nagging heat and the stubborn blood-sucking leeches clinging to our jungle fatigues.

Finally we reached our objective: a small dirt trail we suspected was a well-used footpath for enemy troops. We hastily finished our C-ration meal before nightfall. We ran wire across the trail and connected it to several claymore mines hoping we could score a successful hit while we slept. I found a spot under a tall teak tree and flattened some weeds to make a bed. I spread my green poncho on the ground, unloaded my gear, and tried to catch a decent night's rest before moving out again the next morning.

The tropical, dark jungle on a moonless night was magical. The trees echoed with the sounds of insects and snakes interspersed with the howling of nocturnal predators at a distance. It was a natural symphony, playing a lullaby for the weary souls of my squad and the enemy lurking somewhere in the nearby jungle. The beautiful nature of the surroundings never takes sides, neither had it pitched one against another. It was the hatred and hostility of human nature that turned this once peaceful landscape into a bloody battlefield.

Heavy rain began at midnight. The sudden downpour drove me out of my sleep. Quickly I tried to wrap the poncho around me, cover my gear and go back to sleep again. But the rain kept pouring into my makeshift shelter. I might as well have been lying in a streambed. I could no longer lie down on the ground so I got up and sat against the tree. My body shivered as the cold rain soaked through my uniform. The cold rain splashed on my face, keeping me from falling back to sleep. There was nothing else I could do except stare at the downpour as the flashes of lightning brightened the dark wood around me.

How did I become wrapped up in the madness of this war? I was born in Vietnam where, as long as I could remember, the sound of gunfire and explosions often woke me from my innocent dreams. I had tried every possible avenue to avoid the South Vietnamese draft, but despite my efforts I ended up on one of the worst battlefields in this unpopular war. Every minute of surviving on the battlefield was considered a miracle. I shouldn't even think about what my future would hold. I sometimes came close to convincing myself that I was defending the country where I was born so someday my family could live in peace and prosperity. Without fail, this ideal evaporated in the face of all the destruction, death and injustice I had seen.

Here I was, supposedly fighting for the freedom of my homeland, yet I had become a slave of a war with no end in sight. Each of us enlisted in the ARVN without term limit — to serve until we were either wounded, killed, decided to desert, or for as long as the war demanded. Many of my friends had good careers or had fled the country at the onset of the war. They were enjoying their lives while I was stuck in this dark jungle searching for an elusive enemy.

Looking into the pitch black above me I cried out to God, *"Why can't I have a life like my friends? How soon can I be free to live a normal life, without war, poverty, or misery? What was the purpose of my existence? Was I born just to face a senseless death?"* My questions hung in thin air without answers that night as I sat, drenched, under the tall teak tree in the dark jungle.

I felt a light tap on my shoulder. I had fallen asleep and I opened my eyes to the bright morning light. The rain had stopped long ago. I packed up my gear and moved out again.

Part One

The Horrors of War

Those who live in the shelter of the Most High
will find rest in the shadow of the Almighty.

This I declare of the Lord:
He alone is my refuge, my place of safety;
he is my God, and I am trusting him.

He will shield you with his wings.
He will shelter you with his feathers.
His faithful promises are your armor and protection.

Do not be afraid of the terrors of the night,
nor the fear the dangers of the day,
nor dread the plague that stalks in darkness,
nor the disaster that strikes at midday.

Though a thousand fall at your side,
though ten thousand are dying around you,
these evils will not touch you.

The Lord says, "I will rescue those who love me.
I will protect those who trust in my name.

When they call on me, I will answer;
I will be with them in trouble.
I will rescue them and honor them.

Excerpts from Psalm 91 (NLT)

– CHAPTER 1 –

My Family

I am the third child in a family of twelve children, two girls and ten boys. My father, Dang, migrated from Quangzhou Province, China, to Saigon, Vietnam, in September 1940, to work as a textile worker. He was a quiet and humble person and stood less than five feet tall. Nevertheless, his industriousness and ingenuity made him a giant in my eyes. In 1946, the year I was born, my father took out all of his savings to start a small textile factory. Instead of using a traditional, hand-operated weaver, he designed a motorized weaver that automatically controlled the warp and weft threads of a silk loom using a pattern box attached to a string of pre-punched paper cards mounted on top of the weaver. This allowed him to create high-quality, complex, custom designs on the clothing product. In those days his weaver was considered the most technologically advanced piece of textile machinery in that part of the world.

Initially he installed several of the newly-designed machines in the front half of the house. Soon his business was booming. He rented an additional building nearby and bought more equipment to expand his business. He hired workers to keep up with the domestic demand and even exported finished goods to neighboring Cambodia. He became a well-known consultant of his trade. In those golden years of his life he was highly respected among his competitors in the textile business.

A master of his trade, my father enjoyed hiring young apprentices to pass down his skill, giving them a chance to excel. He treated his employees with dignity and fairness. Every year, a few days before the Chinese Lunar New Year Festival (Vietnamese call *Tet*), we would gather outside his office to watch as he proudly handed out hefty bonuses to his workers before they left for a well-deserved New Year's vacation.

My mother, Kieu, was raised in my father's hometown. As a teenager she accompanied her two elder sisters on a journey to Saigon to escape starvation. She was a typical Chinese, rural village woman — hardworking, strong-backed, illiterate, loving and kind.

My mother's entire life revolved around taking care of her children and family. While my father was busy running his business barely having time for his children, my mother had to bear most of the responsibilities in raising her ever-expanding family, taking us to school, preparing three meals a day and doing house chores. Evenings usually involved her watching vigilantly as we all sat around the dinner table to do our homework, despite the fact that she did not know how to read or write. Her greatest regret in life was that she could not read and write (back in those days, the traditional Chinese family did not send girls to school). Because of this painful stigma, she vowed to never allow her children to be illiterate. Every time any of us skipped homework or came home with low grades on our report card, she spanked us as she wept, reminding us of the pain she had endured.

Though she could not read, she certainly knew how to count. At meal time, instead of remembering a dozen names of her children, it was much easier to count how many heads showed up at the dinner table.

"This is the only way not to leave out anyone!" she sometimes moaned.

"Who is missing?" She always asked. Then we all tried to help her figure it out. She searched around the neighbors until everyone was accounted for before saying grace and starting the meal. Feeding a family of twelve kids in those days was expensive. She was always the last one to eat. Often she would scrape the burned rice from the bottom of the rice pot for herself.

We lived in a decent row house on Uu Long Street south of downtown Cho Lon, the Chinese section of Saigon. Our neighborhood consisted mostly of other Chinese expatriates and was generally peaceful. However, down the street there was a small band of young teenagers my mother nicknamed "The Yellow Bullies" because their leader often wore a yellow t-shirt. They were boys who usually loitered after school at a corner down the street and often harassed me and my neighborhood friends when we were on our way home from school.

"Don't mess around with these Yellow Bully gangsters!" my mother warned. "Stay as far away from them as you can."

I could not put up with this anymore. One day I banded with a few kids in my neighborhood and formed an alliance to protect our turf and challenge the Yellow Bullies. I remember one hot Saturday afternoon after school, as I and other boys were playing marbles on the street, the Yellow Bullies marched into our neighborhood to pick a fight. My loose alliance of neighborhood children rushed to confront them with rocks and sticks. Soon rocks flew and kids shouted, and our small, quiet neighborhood became a miniature battlefield. My mother heard the commotion and rushed outside, an old apron still hanging from her waist. She soon found me in the midst of the bruised, bloodied gaggle of boys. She grasped my left ear, dragged me into the house and closed the front door. I knew I was in trouble.

"I told you many times not to mess with these thugs!" she screamed at me as she took out a long stick made of solid rattan with a few chicken feathers still glued at one end.

"These kids came to pick a fight — we were just defending ourselves!" I protested as I started crying and stamping my feet.

"I do not care who started the fight. When you get into a fight, you get punished. I only discipline my own children, let the other mothers take care of their own."

She made me turn around as I continued to plead for mercy.

Whack! Whack! The whipping sound was coming from behind me. Instantly I felt sharp pain shooting from my rear end up my spine. I cried for a while, still protesting the injustice. She made me stand alone at the corner behind the living room window until the evening meal was ready.

In 1954, my one-year-old brother Thach suddenly developed a high fever and died in my father's arms. One year later, my four-year-old sister Siu was playing near the weaving machine in our house. She accidentally placed her left hand between the gears of a weaving machine and severed several of her fingers. My parents took her to the hospital, but two weeks later she died of tetanus. A year after my sister died, my four-month-old baby brother, Cuong, died of an unknown disease in the hospital. These consecutive tragedies shocked my whole family to the core, and it seemed a dark cloud had fallen. For the first time I was confronted with the fear of my own mortality. Could I be next? Why did these tragedies happen to my family? Though my parents called themselves Christians, they seldom went to church. My father was busy with his business and seldom had time to attend church services. My mother was so busy managing her large family that she could hardly keep track of the days of the week. She frequently asked us to remind her of the first Sunday of the month so that she could go to church for communion.

These tragic events became a turning point for my family's spiritual life. My father decided to take us to Sunday school. Every Saturday night, after a long day's work, the whole family would gather together to sing and pray. Our neighbors knew we were Christians because we were the only house on the street to celebrate Christmas. On Christmas day my mother baked cakes and goodies to treat our neighbors. A three-foot-tall artificial Christmas tree sat on a wood bench in our tiny living room, decorated with a solitary string of colored lights and shiny silver tinsel. There were no ornaments or gifts under the tree. The tree piqued the curiosity of the neighborhood children. Neighbors gathered in front of our house just to see the decorations. Even those boys who once were part of the Yellow Bullies came over to enjoy the festivities. We had grown up somewhat and decided to abandon our silly, petty, gang-banging behavior and became close friends. It was truly peace on earth and good will toward men.

When I was 14, the year I finished grade school, my father's business faltered when political strife between Vietnam and Cambodia arose. The two countries severed diplomatic ties and closed the border. This sudden change of events caught my father off-guard. Unable to export his textile products to Cambodia and short on cash, while most of the finished goods sat idly in the warehouse, he had no choice but to shut down half of the factory, lay off all the workers, and consolidate his weaver machines to the already overcrowded house. The hardest part for my father was to let go of many of his hard-working employees whom he had trained and treated as if they were his own sons. At that time, our family had grown to nine children, with more on the way. My father thought about changing careers, but as a business owner without capital and the head of a large family, he had no other choice but to keep his business running.

One day my father gathered us at the dining table. He told my older brother Alex, my sister Mai, and I that he no longer could afford for us to go to school and that he needed us to work in his factory. Alex insisted that he would get a scholarship from his school to continue his education, which he eventually did. However, Mai and I had no other way but to quit school and work in the family business.

Family photo, 1963. Back row (l.-r.) — Mai, Alex, Daniel, Benson.
Front row (l.-r.) — Marvin, Mother, Jason, Thomas, Andrew, Dad, Tony.

Early one morning I passed Phuc Kien High School on the way
to make a delivery to a customer. Students my age dressed in neat,
white shirts and khaki pants were playing happily on the playground,
some buying food and drinks from the roadside hawkers before class.
I stopped at a corner to watch them from a distance. I felt as if something had been ripped away from me. Watching them, I felt the full
weight of being denied the privilege to learn and to live like a normal
teenager. I felt tears rolling down my cheek. I had no control over my
father's financial woes much less the political strife between Vietnam
and Cambodia. Yet here I was watching my peers living a life that I
should have had. Life was not fair. I wiped my tears and returned to
work.

I continued my secondary education in evening school. After eight
hours of work I would spend one hour doing homework on the roof
of my house. At the far end of the rooftop, facing south, was a large,

wooden dormer window providing a cool, shady place from the blazing sun on a hot summer afternoon. It became my sanctuary from my father's noisy machines and from my younger brothers' constant frenzy around the overcrowded house. Sometimes I laid there watching the sun set over the horizon, thinking what my future would be like. I realized my only hope to break away from the vicious cycle of poverty was through education.

Alex and I both loved reading. We read everything we could put our hands on. We loved to explore new ideas and delve into world history and politics. In those days there was no decent library in Cho Lon. The only place to find good, bargain books was the used-book stores along Phung Hung Street near the main marketplace. Often Alex and I spent weekend hours rummaging through piles of smelly, old books to find a few that looked fascinating. Once in a while we would trade in the books we finished for other titles. Our favorite reading materials were writings of famous philosophers such as Plato, Aristotle, and Descartes.

As communism, socialism and increased U.S. involvement in Vietnam became hot topics in the local newspaper in the early 1960s, we looked for books on the doctrines of Karl Marx and Friedrich Engels (which were considered contraband material at that time), as well as the history of the United States of America and the doctrines of democracy and capitalism. The ideals of democracy, liberty and justice resonated in my young mind, and I dreamt that one day I could leave my war-torn country for America.

Though I was raised in a Christian family, I had no interest in going to church at all. My Sunday school teacher, Mrs. Chan, was loving and caring. She kept coming to my house to share the gospel stories with me when I did not show up at her class. Eventually I started paying attention to the salvation that Jesus Christ had brought to me on the cross. I finally realized that Christianity is not a religion as I first thought. Rather, it is a personal relationship with God our Creator so that we can be saved and find the purpose of life. So one day, when I was sixteen years old, I committed my life to the Lord as my Savior in my Sunday school class.

In the Bible there are more than 360 verses telling us God has called us not to be afraid because He promises to be with us in any circumstance we encounter. My future was in the hands of the Almighty God who controls the history of mankind. Why should I be afraid?

CHAPTER 2

A Brief History
of Indochina Wars

In order to fully understand the circumstances of my life as the Vietnam War evolved, let me take you on a brief history of the conflict and U.S. military involvement.

At the end of WWII, French Indochina (now Laos, Cambodia and Vietnam) fell into a political power vacuum as Japanese forces surrendered and abandoned the land. Meanwhile, the French Union force was crippled and weak after the war and soon lost control of the region. Viet Minh (League for the Independence of Vietnam), led by Ho Chi Minh, seized the opportunity to launch the so-called "August Revolution." On September 2, 1945, he declared the independence of Democratic Republic of Vietnam before a crowd of 500,000 people in Hanoi's Ba Dinh Square. He even asked the United States for help to rebuild his country from its ruin. However, the principal allied victors of WWII (Britain, the Soviet Union and the United States) insisted that Indochina belonged to the French as a colony. Since the French were not able to govern Vietnam, the Allies came to an agreement that British troops would occupy the South while Chang Kai Shek's Chinese Nationalist forces took over the North.[1]

Ho Chi Minh initially attempted to negotiate with the French government to allow Vietnam to become an independent state, but the

French government would not budge. In January 1946, Viet Minh won elections across central and northern Vietnam.[1] In March, the French Union force landed in Hanoi to reclaim the city. In November of that year they ousted Viet Minh from the city. Soon thereafter, Viet Minh began launching a guerrilla war against the French occupation. This was the beginning of the First Indochina War.

On May 7, 1954, Viet Minh, with crucial support from the Soviet Union and the People's Republic of China, handed the French force a stunning military defeat in the battle of Dien Bien Phu, marking the end of French involvement in Indochina. At the Geneva Conference, France negotiated a cease-fire agreement with Viet Minh, which included independence for Laos, Cambodia and Vietnam.[2]

Under the terms of the Geneva Convention, Vietnam was temporarily partitioned at the 17th parallel in central Vietnam. Civilians were to be given the opportunity to move freely between the two transitional states.[1] Elections throughout the country were to be held later compliant to the Geneva Accords. Fearing persecution by the communists, about one million northerners, predominantly Catholic Christians, fled south with the help of U.S. Navy ships. It is estimated that as many as more than two million would have left had they not been stopped by the Viet Minh.[2]

Viet Minh established a communist state in the North and engaged in a radical land reform program in which an estimated 8,000 so called "class enemies" were executed. Political purging and famine plagued the North for many years to come.[1]

Meanwhile, a non-communist state was established in the South under Emperor Bao Dai, a former puppet of the French and Japanese.[2] Ngo Dinh Diem was appointed as his prime minister. While the Catholic Christians fled south, a 130,000-man Viet Minh force withdrew to North Vietnam as *Tap Ket* (Revolutionary Regroupees) anticipating a return to the South within two years for an armed struggle to unify the country. Viet Minh also left approximately 5,000 to 10,000 armed cadres in South Vietnam as part of the "political-military" infrastructure with the intention of laying the groundwork for retaking the South when the time came. These trained revolutionaries would eventually make up the core of the Viet Cong.

While Ngo Dinh Diem was trying to consolidate his power in the South, he ran up against a powerful, well-armed criminal and racketeering organization called "Binh Xuyen," which controlled the city of Saigon and Cho Lon territory for many years. Binh Xuyen first emerged in the early 1920s as pirate gangs in the marshes and canals along the southern fringes of Saigon-Cho Lon. They extorted protection money from the sampans and junks that traveled the canals on their way to deliver food supply at the Cho Lon docks.[3] Under the leadership of Ba Duong and Le Van Vien (who was also known as Bay Vien), they turned a small band of 200-300 criminals into a well-equipped army of 10,000. In the early 1930s and 1940s they were hunted by the French colonial army, and in 1941 Le Van Vien was captured and imprisoned in Con Son until he escaped early in 1945. By the mid 1950s Binh Xuyen dominated the Saigon underworld.

During WWII, Le Van Vien and his band collaborated with the Japanese forces in Indochina to overthrow the French colonial administration. As a result, he was installed as a police official to the newly-established Japanese occupation government. As WWII came to an abrupt end in August 1945, Japan surrendered. The French forces returned to Indochina and began to clear the Viet Minh out of Saigon and searched house to house for their leaders. Realizing the support of Binh Xuyen was crucial to their struggle in the South, the Viet Minh convinced Ba Duong and Le Van Nguyen to align with them against the French. However, the alliance did not last long. The division was not of any ideological disputes, but rather trivial fighting over discipline, behavior, and territorial control.

After the French forced the Viet Minh to retreat from the city, the French saw Binh Xuyen as a unique urban counterintelligence and security force. So a criminal organization became an invaluable asset to the French in supporting their presence in the region. They decided to turn over the twin cities of Saigon and Cho Lon block by block to the Binh Xuyen gangs.

Besides using Binh Xuyen to keep the Viet Minh out, the French colonial government also allowed these gangsters to plunder the cities to finance their colonial operation in Indochina. Soon Le Van Vien was promoted to general and commander of the police headquarters in Saigon.[3] Binh Xuyen was awarded the lucrative franchise of two main casinos: Grand Monde and Cloche D'Oo. They organized lottery concessions, operated opium processing plants, and distributed opium to hundreds of dens throughout the city. They also owned and operated many brothels in the city. In fact, when the Hall of Mirrors, the largest brothel in Asia, opened its doors, French officials presided over the dedication ceremony. Binh Xuyen also became the tax collection agency for the colonial government and often extorted money for merchants in the twin cities.

Ngo Dinh Diem realized he had no choice but to use force to disband the Binh Xuyen gangs. Tension mounted and the two sides fortified their defensive positions in the city to prepare for an imminent battle. The fighting began March 27, 1955, when one of Diem's elite paratrooper companies attacked the police headquarters in Saigon controlled by Binh Xuyen. To counter this attack, the Binh Xuyen shelled the presidential palace the following day. The exchange of fire lasted for two days until the French tanks rolled into the city to impose a cease fire.

The house where I lived was in the Xom Cui area, south of Cho Lon. My neighborhood had been firmly under the control of Binh Xuyen since my father moved there in early 1943. The area was sandwiched between two canals. Every day on my way to and from school I had to cross Chai Gia Bridge. On the afternoon of May 2, 1955, as I was on my way home from school, I noticed many green beret-wearing Binh Xuyen soldiers taking positions on the bridge and the high-rise buildings along the canal. For a nine-year-old boy, I had no idea what this was all about and I played outside my house with my friends as usual. Suddenly I heard several explosions shake the whole neighborhood. Black smoke billowed several blocks from my house followed by the sounds of machine gun and small arms fire. I saw my father running toward the house screaming, "Get inside the house!"

He rushed us inside and shut the door. We gathered in the back of the house as my mom hastily prepared supper over a wood stove. After the meal, my father instructed all of us to stay under a hardwood plank bed while he gathered furniture and other materials available in the house to fortify our improvised shelter. Overnight the fighting intensified. Sounds of explosions kept me from falling asleep and I heard the rumble of heavy boots running outside the house. The Binh Xuyen troops were setting up positions along my street.

The next morning the fighting was not as intense as the night before. I peeked through a crack in a window. I saw troops still manning their positions, smoke darkening the sky and ash filling the air. The straw huts in the slum on the other side of the canal behind my house had been set on fire. My father was turned away when he tried to venture down the street.

We stayed in the shelter in my house for another night. The next morning things seemed unusually quiet. My father opened the door to find our neighbors fleeing the war zone. He, too, decided it was time for us to evacuate. We packed clothing and belongings and headed toward the bridge. The buildings on both sides of the canal were severely damaged and some were still burning. Not a single Binh Xuyen gang was in sight. Weakened by years of corruption, the Binh Xuyen bandits were no longer the tough guerrillas of a decade before.[3]

Apparently they had abandoned their positions overnight.

Along the bridge, many of Diem's Armed Forces of the Republic of Vietnam (ARVN) soldiers were heading toward the battlefield while thousands of frightened civilians like us were fleeing in the opposite direction. Finally, we reached my uncle Thuan To's house on Tan Hung street a few miles away from the war zone. A week later the Binh Xuyen gang was defeated and retreated into the depths of the Rung Sat Swamp south of Saigon.[3] The battle left more than 500 civilians dead, 2,000 wounded and up to 50,000 homeless.

In 1961, as Ngo Dinh Diem consolidated his power in the south, North Vietnam began sending the Revolutionary Regroupees back to the south to launch an armed struggle. The National Liberation Front (NLF) of South Vietnam was formally established. Members of this organization were commonly called Viet Cong. Communist forces in the Vietnam War consisted of the North Vietnamese Army (NVA) and the Viet Cong (VC). The Viet Cong soldiers were mainly Southerners who aligned with them.

Ngo Dinh Diem, a staunch Nationalist Catholic, in fear of a Communist victory, rejected the general election which was to be held across the country under the terms of the Geneva Accord. Instead, he held a rigged referendum to declare himself as President of the Republic of Vietnam. He created an authoritarian government mainly comprised of his family members. His brother Ngo Dinh Nhu became his political advisor and head of a secret police force called "Thanh Nien Cong Hoa" (The Republican Youth). He also formed a political party named "Dang Can Lao" to support Diem's regime. His sister-in-law, Madame Nhu, was the most powerful woman in the country. His brother Ngo Dinh Can was put in charge of the city of Hue, Ngo Dinh

Thuc became archbishop of Hue and Ngo Dinh Luyen the ambassador to the United Kingdom.[4]

In early 1963, after subduing the Binh Xuyen organized crime gangsters, Ngo Dinh Diem turned against Cao Dai, a syncretistic religion established in Tay Ninh Province. In May that year, Diem's government prohibited the Buddhist majority to fly the Buddhist flag in the city of Hue in central Vietnam during Vesak celebrations that commemorated the birth of Gautama Buddha. A riot broke out and nine unarmed civilians were killed. Soon the protests spread into other major cities. Ngo Dinh Diem sent his troops to raid Buddhist temples, firing into anti-government demonstrators on the street and arresting monks and dissidents. The opposition grew. Many monks went on hunger strikes, and a few set themselves on fire in the busy streets of Saigon. Many university students joined in protest against the repressive regime. Daily riots spread from Saigon to Cho Lon where I lived. The unrest plagued the city for more than a year.

Outraged by the Diem regime's repressive policies, the Kennedy administration in Washington, D.C., contacted South Vietnamese military leaders that the United States would be willing to support a regime change, noting they would not punish anyone involved in the removal of President Diem. On the morning of November 1, 1963, the South Vietnamese Army, led by Gen. Duong Van Minh (Big Minh) and five other army generals, mobilized their troops to launch a coup. The rebel troops surrounded the president's palace and demanded both President Diem and his brother Nhu to surrender. By nightfall, Diem and Nhu and their entourage escaped through an underground passage and took refuge in Cha Tam Catholic Church in Cho Lon, which was located not far from my school. The next morning, a convoy of military armored vehicles arrived at the church. Both brothers were arrested and immediately executed inside one of the armored personnel carriers parked outside of the church. When I heard the news of their death, the whole city was in shock. Yes, many celebrated the end of the authoritarian regime, but we were also shaken by the brutal execution of a national leader without a reasonable cause.

Did they not first deserve a fair trial if they had committed any crime against their people? Nevertheless, Diem was by far the strongest Nationalist and anti-Communist leader Vietnam ever had. Interestingly enough, less than three weeks after their deaths, President John F. Kennedy was assassinated in Dallas, Texas. On that day, some newspapers circulating on the streets of Saigon reported that *Ong Troi* (Heaven) had revenge for the death of their leader.

– CHAPTER 3 –

Turning Point

The death of Ngo Dinh Diem was the main turning point of the Vietnam War. Following the coup, chaos plagued the nation. North Vietnam and the Viet Cong in the south took advantage of the chaos to step up insurgent activities in an attempt to gain control of the south. South Vietnam fell into a period of extreme political instability as one military regime overthrew another in quick succession. No one was sure who the legitimate leader of the country was anymore. In August 1965, after two years of political turmoil, a unified National Leadership Committee was established and appointed a general named Nguyen Van Thieu to be the chairman. Two years later, South Vietnamese ratified a new constitution. A general election was held in September. The same year, Nguyen Van Thieu was elected as the president of the second Republic of Vietnam.

In 1963 there were 16,300 U.S. military advisors training the Armed Forces of the Republic of Vietnam (ARVN) soldiers. They were part of the American effort to prepare the ARVN to fight the war themselves. They even accompanied them on operations deep inside enemy territory. As the situation deteriorated and American casualties began to mount, newly sworn-in President Lyndon B. Johnson worried not only that the situation could get out of control, but also that if Vietnam fell to Communism, other countries in Asia would follow. As the

Viet Cong grew stronger, it seemed impossible to win the war with weak and corrupt ARVN forces. In August 1964, the USS Maddox and USS Turner Joy were allegedly attacked by North Vietnamese navy gunboats in the Gulf of Tonkin. This prompted the U.S. Congress to pass the Gulf of Tonkin Resolution giving the president authority to launch military operations in Southeast Asia without declaring war.[1]

On March 2, 1965, U.S. bombers began waging air raid campaigns over North Vietnam and on Ho Chi Minh Trail. The famous trail, in fact, was a camouflaged highway that ran across the border of Laos and Cambodia for delivering military equipment and supplies to support NVA troops in the south. In order to protect the Da Nang Air base in central Vietnam, more than 2,000 U.S. marines landed south of Da Nang on March 8, 1965. This marked the beginning of the U.S. ground war in Vietnam, also called the Second Indochina War, and commonly called the Vietnam War.[1]

As the fighting intensified, war deaths mounted. Funeral processions for deceased ARVN soldiers became a common scene on the streets of Saigon. Newspapers were filled with obituaries of military deaths. Fear gripped the citizens of the city. Business was severely affected due to the Viet Cong's sabotage efforts along the countryside. They also cut off major roads causing food shortages in the city. Every night, as I lay in bed, I could hear the sound of small arms fire and explosions in the distance. Sporadic fighting was at the capital's doorstep.

Many of my richer neighbors sent their young men overseas to avoid the military draft. Some of my friends were drafted into the ARVN forces only to desert after a few months of basic training. My close friend Trong Binh Lu, who was a few years older than I was, was sent to the battlefield after he completed basic training. One day, a soldier came to his parents' home to inform them to come to the military morgue and receive his body — he was killed in action only one month after he was sent to the battlefield.

War made my future uncertain. My ideal life — getting an education, finding a decent job, settling down, getting married and raising a family — was no longer clearly possible. I was about to be drafted and my dreams for the future were fading as war crept ever closer into my life.

It was April 20, 1967, the year I turned 20, like every young man in the country, I was drafted into the ARVN.

Because I learned to speak English well during high school and from the American missionaries at my church, I was selected to serve as a military interpreter to U.S. armed forces in Vietnam. After three months of military basic training, I attended the military linguistic school in Saigon. One morning, two weeks into my English study, I was called to the office.

"Sgt. Tinh (my Vietnamese name), I know your English is sufficient. Therefore, you have completed your course," said the 1st lieutenant in charge of the linguistic program. "You pack up tomorrow and get ready to go to the battlefield."

"Sir, I only have been here for two weeks. I'm not ready yet!" I protested.

"You will be fine! You can learn the rest in the unit. Besides, we are short of interpreters on the front lines."

So I graduated the next day with the rank of sergeant-first class.

My first assignment was at the 5th ARVN Infantry Division headquarters in Phu Loi, Binh Duong Province. Later I was transferred to Chon Thanh District in Binh Long Province.

I did not have the faintest idea about Chon Thanh district until I mentioned it to my comrade, Lt. Nguyen Van Tam, a veteran officer serving at the division's intelligence (G2) office at that time. When I told him I was transferred to Chon Thanh, he pulled me aside.

"Tinh, I'm worried about you. If you go there, you will not come back alive."

"Why?" I was not convinced.

"Tinh, I know it is unfair to you. Nobody wants to go to Chon Thanh. That is why they are sending you there. If I were you, I'd rather pay somebody off to get a better assignment, or just desert before you report for duty. In case you need help, I can talk to my superior."

"Paying somebody off? I'm not going to do it!" I insisted. "How could I take my family's hard-earned money to satisfy those corrupt officers?" I knew Lt. Tam was sincerely trying to help me (he had lost several of his friends in battles near Chon Thanh), but I had no money to pay. Besides, I would rather fight VC in the jungle than satisfy the greed of ARVN officers. I joined the army in part because I felt it was my duty to defend the freedom of my country where I was born and because of the political knowledge I had gained over the years. I knew well what a communist regime could do to this country should they take over the South.

Undeniably, corruption was an open secret in the ARVN. Army commanders demanded bribes from new recruits, particularly from ethnic Chinese soldiers whose parents could afford the payment. A small amount could land someone like me in an assignment doing office work in the comfortable rear base in Saigon. A larger sum could put my name on a ghost payroll so I would never have to report for duty at all.

I went home to tell my parents that I would be leaving the next day for my new assignment. My father sensed something was not right, but he understood that there was not much he could do either. My mother did not take the news well. I watched her face fall as I told her. She slumped into a rattan chair without saying a word. I walked over and sat beside her.

She looked at me with teary eyes, and touched my face with her calloused hand. I felt the trembling. "I wish they would take me instead." She sounded like a helpless hen watching one of her chicks being snatched away by a vulture.

"Mom, don't be silly. I'm all grown up now. I can take care of myself. You just have to pray for me more often." I put my hand on her frail shoulder. "Besides, Chon Thanh is only a three hours' bus ride from home. I promise I will come home as often as possible to see you."

"Do you promise? Don't make me worry about you." She nodded reluctantly, as she wiped her tears.

"Yes, Mom, I promise."

I watched her frail figure walk slowly back to the kitchen.

I never forgot what I promised my mother. I knew that as a soldier my primary responsibility was to follow the army's orders and I would have to set my family priorities aside. Nevertheless, for the next three years while serving in Chon Thanh, I tried to come home to see my mother, even if it meant going AWOL for a few hours on the weekends. I did all of this thinking I would lessen her burden if she could see that I was, at the very least, alive. She already had more than she could bear just taking care of her family, and I tried my best to keep her from worrying about me.

Many years later my sister Mai told me that my mother often wept when she rinsed the rice for dinner because one of her sons would not be at the table that day.

I could not sleep that night. I kept thinking about the pain I might cause my parents. Nevertheless, I took comfort that I still had many brothers who would care for them if anything happened to me on the battlefield. At least I was at peace and no longer afraid of what lay ahead for me. Now everything was in God's hands.

The next morning I packed my gear, some clothing and food for the road. My father gathered the whole family in the living room to say goodbye to me. He prayed: "Dear Lord. You know we cannot do anything for Tinh, and I ask you to protect him and bring him home safe. Amen."

He turned away with tears in his eyes.

– CHAPTER 4 –

Chon Thanh

Binh Long province was located 65 miles north of Saigon and consisted of three districts: Loc Ninh in the north, Chon Thanh in the south, and An Loc, the provincial capital, sandwiched between. The province was well known for its red, fertile soil suitable for growing rubber trees and had prospered for many years. Binh Long means "peace and prosperity," but now it was anything but peaceful. Its 40,000 residents had seen their fair share of war since the early 1960s. The province bordered Cambodia to the north where the North Vietnamese Army (NVA) had major sanctuary camps and supply depots. The NVA often conducted hit-and-fade raids throughout Binh Long and then retreated to their sanctuaries to regroup and resupply.

I arrived in Chon Thanh by helicopter on a sunny morning in October 1967. Even from the air it was obvious this small town of 7,000 was the frontline of a war without a battlefront. As the helicopter circled over the town approaching the airstrip, I could see many large bomb craters littering the landscape like honeycombs. They were less than two miles from either side of the highway running through the middle of the town.

Located 45 miles north of Saigon, Chon Thanh was situated strategically between War Zone C to the west and War Zone D to the east. It was one of the most volatile regions during the Vietnam War.

National highway QL-13 was a main traffic artery connecting Saigon to Cambodia and beyond during the time it had all been part of French Indochina. It was the main road through An Loc, Loc Ninh, Quan Loi Base, Binh Phuoc and other adjacent small towns.

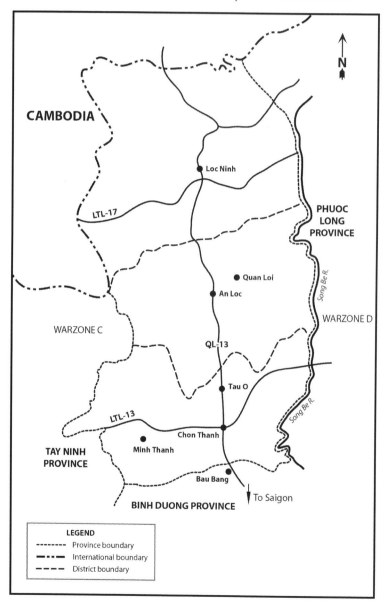

When I first arrived, the stretch of QL-13 from Lai Khe to An Loc was a two-lane, unpaved dirt road. It got the nicknames "Mine Alley" and "Thunder Road" because the Viet Cong often placed mines during the night and ambushed military convoys in daylight. To combat this, U.S. Rome Plow teams (engineer teams that used a specially-modified armored bulldozers) cleared 200 meters of jungle vegetation on both sides of the road, and U.S. and South Vietnamese minesweepers went on patrol every morning. Despite this effort, mine incidents still happened often on this stretch of the road. Whenever a convoy was ambushed or when civilian buses accidentally tripped a land mine, the dirty job of cleaning up the mess was given to the district's paramilitary units. They pulled charred corpses from mangled autos, gathered bloody body parts that were scattered around the scene, and then towed the bus away leaving the crater for others to patch up. It was not until late 1969 that the U.S. Army Corps of Engineers finally reconstructed this stretch of QL-13 with asphalt pavement which dramatically reduced land mine incidents.

There were three Thunder Fire Support Bases (FSBs), one located north of Bau Bang and one south of Tau-O. The other one was on the east side of the district compound. Since 1967, the 1/4th Calvary Regiment, then 1st Infantry Division, and the armor unit of the 11th Armor Cavalry Regiment had consecutively manned these bases. Their primary mission was to provide security for this stretch of the road and firepower for military operations in the area.

Chon Thanh's marketplace, situated on the west side of QL-13, was a small, tin roof-covered building with a yellowish wood frame structure and a bullet ridden façade. Its impromptu fresh food stalls stretched almost 50 yards to the sidewalk of the road. Several restaurants and roadside cafés sprung up on both sides of the busy street to cater to the soldiers stationed nearby. The marketplace was also a popular place for U.S. troops. American GIs sometimes stopped by for a bottle of cold lager the locals called "Biere 33." Next to the market-place was the power station that housed a small, 200-kilowatt generator to supply electricity to the town. The generator ran for only three hours after dusk each day. Since the generator was the only touch of modern life in town, it became a frequent target during the years I was there. A local paramilitary squad set up a permanent post to protect this generator.

I was stationed at the district compound at the south end of the town. Previously a U.S. Special Forces camp, it was turned over to the local government and now served as the district administration office and military headquarters and the U.S. Military Advisory Team 47 compound. To the south were the ARVN 7th Infantry Regiment headquarters and an all-weather steel plank airstrip parallel to QL-13. A Regional Force (RF) company was the primary defender of the district compound. The U.S. advisory team shared responsibility to defend part of the north side of the perimeter. Since the compound was a confluence of South Vietnamese and American interests, it became a constant target for the enemy. Even before I arrived in early September 1967, defensive positions of the compound had long been put in place. By early 1968, with the help of the U.S. Army Corp of Engineers, the district dug a 20-foot-wide by 10-foot-deep trench surrounding the compound. In addition, they installed additional barbed wire fences along the outer perimeter.

I stayed at the U.S. military advisor quarters and dined in their mess hall which was considered a luxury among Vietnamese soldiers. My primary job was to translate communiqués and documents that traveled between Vietnamese and U.S. forces. It was a 24/7 job, and I was constantly on call for anything that happened within the district. U.S. District Advisory Teams usually consisted of a senior advisor (usually an Army captain or major), one lieutenant as his assistant, a non-commissioned officer, a medic and a radio operator. Their primary function was to coordinate activities with the local government, paramilitary Regional Force/Popular Force (RF/PF) units, ARVN units, and U.S. military forces operating in the district. In addition, they provided training and equipment to the RF/PF and accompanied them on patrol and reconnaissance operations within the district.

My first superior was Capt. Thomas Gallagher, an Illinois native. He walked as if he was marching in a parade but at a much faster pace. With my short legs, I had a hard time keeping up with him. He was a well-disciplined army officer, always dressed in iron-pressed, green jungle fatigues, and a hardcore workaholic who took his job seriously. As his interpreter, I hardly had any time to rest. He and I were constantly on the move from daybreak to midnight visiting villages, providing food and farm equipment to refugees, training the district paramilitary units in weaponry and warfare, and arranging dust-offs (medical evacuation helicopters) for seriously ill civilians and wounded soldiers. After nightfall we would often set up ambushes in the nearby jungle with the district paramilitary units. The next morning, after a stressful night of watching for the enemy (and the occasional firefight), we would go back to our day jobs.

Despite long hours and hard work, I enjoyed what I was doing because I could see before my eyes that our efforts had turned the tide in contested areas once controlled by the enemy. Now that they were in the hands of the South Vietnamese government, the locals were given a chance to live a normal life.

January 31, 1968, was the first day of the Tet festival. It was part of the Lunar New Year and the most celebrated holiday in Asia. A week earlier, both the NVA and ARVN announced a three-day cease fire to honor the festival. Everyone, it seemed, needed a break from this endless war.

On the eve of Tet, I received a three-day pass to go home and celebrate with my family. It was the first time I returned home since I arrived in Chon Thanh. I took a military helicopter flight to Tan Son Nhut Airport in Saigon and then hailed a cab to my home in Cho Lon. The city was in a celebratory mood — the street was bustling with cars, scooters, and streams of pedestrians. The local marketplace overflowed to the side streets with colorful flowers and sweet confection stands. Everyone hurried to finish last minute shopping before the family reunion dinner, a tradition no one wanted to miss.

I arrived home at noon to find my mom busy in the kitchen putting the finishing touches on her famous seven-course dinner. The whole family was coming, including all of my aunts and one uncle.

The celebrations began after dinner that night. Firecrackers rang out in the air, brightening the sky. The neighborhood children joyfully put on their new clothing to welcome the New Year. For some families it was the only time they could afford to buy new clothing for their children. After midnight, many of my neighbors went to a nearby shrine and brought back some burning incense, a Chinese tradition that symbolized bringing peace and prosperity back to the family.

As firecrackers and incense smoke still swirled in the air, NVA and Viet Cong commando units began their surprise attack on several key cities throughout central Vietnam. The enemy smuggled weapons and equipment in shipments of flowers, gifts and food brought in en masse for the New Year celebration. NVA and VC soldiers dressed in civilian clothing used fake IDs and bribery to gain access to Saigon. By dawn, the attack had spread over 100 towns and cities across South Vietnam, as well as all major U.S. military installations and air bases in the area. It was the beginning of the Tet Offensive.

The morning of New Year's Day in Saigon was sunny and blazingly hot. I was going out to visit friends and relatives as part of the New Year tradition. On my way into downtown Saigon I heard the sound of explosions in the distance. Assuming it was the sound of firecrackers, I stayed with my family and continued the traditional walk. Suddenly, I saw two U.S. Cobra gunship helicopters circling overhead and firing on targets below. People started fleeing as black smoke billowed into the sunny sky. This was no firecracker celebration.

I turned around and ran back home. I cranked up the only radio in the house only to hear static coming from the speaker. I headed out again to look for a friend who lived by the Phu Tho race track not far from my house. As I approached the slums near the race track, I found the street packed with people fleeing the area. Some piled their belongings onto their scooters or bicycles, while others fled on foot only carrying their loved ones. A lady in her forties carried her boy in one hand and a sack of clothing in the other. As she walked briskly by, she turned to me and said, "Many Viet Cong are over there!"

I immediately rushed home to find the whole family glued to the radio, listening to an important announcement. President Nguyen Van Thieu had declared martial law and advised citizens to help root out the entrenched enemy. Throughout the day news kept pouring in. The Presidential Palace, ARVN Joint Chiefs of Staff Headquarters, U.S. Embassy compound, Military Assistance Command Vietnam (MACV) Headquarters, Tan Son Nhut Airport, and many other government installations in the capital were attacked by more than five Viet Cong battalions (a total of 1,500-2,000 soldiers). That morning the Saigon national radio station was seized by a Viet Cong commando platoon. They were trying to broadcast a prerecorded message by Ho Chi Minh. However, the cables connecting the station to a relay tower were cut off. It took an ARVN Ranger unit all morning to retake the radio station from enemy control.

Overnight, U.S. aircraft, helicopter gunships, and ARVN armor units continued to pound the enemy positions throughout the city. Heavy fighting took place in my neighborhood in Cho Lon. Viet Cong had turned the vibrant commercial town into a military staging area. The ARVN units had no choice but to bomb the area, setting many houses on fire. I found out later that the slum near the Phu Tho race track was the Viet Cong command post for the offensive in the Saigon region.

The next morning, with sporadic gun battles cropping up throughout the city, the radio station announced that all ARVN soldiers on leave were to report immediately for duty at the nearest military post to join in the defense of the capital. I called Capt. Lu Quang Lam, a good friend of mine stationed at the headquarters of the ARVN Army Corp of Engineers in Saigon. He told me to come in to report for duty and I spent the next two weeks guarding the military installation.

The magnitude and ferocity of the attack had taken both Americans and South Vietnamese by surprise, but their counterattack was ultimately successful. The majority of fighting within the capital was over by February 5. However, it took two more weeks to root out the enemy's entrenched positions in the slums of the Cho Lon area. The communist troops had hoped for a "general uprising" in support of their offensive that never came. Instead, many of the residents of Saigon were angry at the Viet Cong for their deception. In retaliation for breaking the cease fire agreement and disrupting the New Year tradition, the people of Saigon led ARVN troops to Viet Cong hideouts. In the end, the Viet Cong came away from the Tet Offensive with 45,000 dead and 7,000 captured. The U. S. suffered 1,000 casualties and the ARVN lost about 2,300 troops.

The failed offensive decimated the Viet Cong. Not only was their offensive capabilities, command and control infrastructure severely diminished, the morale among their troops was low. From that point on, the NVA had to take over all major fighting efforts. Viet Cong defections increased dramatically in the aftermath of the Tet Offensive.

As the fighting died down in the city, people began to rebuild their homes and livelihoods out of the rubble. I was eager to return to my unit in Chon Thanh. I knew it was unsafe to travel by road, but there was no other choice as the military devoted most of the aircraft for combat operations. I dressed in civilian clothes and took a bus ride from Saigon. As the bus headed north on QL-13, I saw many villages along the road had been burned to the ground. On both sides of the highway hundreds of ARVN soldiers and U.S. armor units pushed deep into the wood to pursue the remnants of the enemy force.

I arrived in Chon Thanh without any incident. To my surprise, Chon Thanh was left untouched by the offensive. Presumably, the VC and NVA units had diverted their attack to the big cities, leaving this small town alone for the time being.

After the Tet Offensive in 1968, the strategy of the Vietnam War changed from "search and destroy" to "clear and hold." Once the U.S. forces and ARVN regular forces swept through enemy-controlled villages, they handed them over to the local RF/PF paramilitary units to secure them. My primary role at that time was to coordinate this effort between the Vietnamese local government and the U.S. units operating in the area.

Winning the hearts and minds of the locals was one of the most crucial tasks of the district administration and its military apparatus. The farmers and woodcutters were the principal source of intelligence. Each day they went into the jungle and returned to the district office with reports of any suspicious enemy activities. In turn, we paid cash for any credible intelligence they could provide. Most of the villagers in the district were devout Catholic, North Vietnamese, anti-communist settlers who fled North Vietnam in 1954 when Ho Chi Minh's Communist regime took over. They were poor but friendly and hardworking. They made their living by logging, farming or working for rubber plantations. Most of them operated one or two charcoal kilns in their backyard to supplement their meager income.

The district advisors were often required to accompany local paramilitary units in conducting patrols in their territory. The operations could last anywhere from two days to one week. The units involved ranged from a small reconnaissance team of five men to an infantry company of 100. The main job of the advisors was to call in fire support in the event the unit made contact with the enemy and to coordinate with U.S. units operating in the area.

I must admit that, at first, I had no confidence in the ARVN forces. I assumed they were corrupt, poorly disciplined and lacking in fighting experience. As I worked with them over the following years, I began to realize they were gradually improving their combat tactics and skills, particularly the local paramilitary RF/PF units with whom I spent so much time conducting combat operations. In fact, they were the ones who were responsible for protecting their native homesteads and their own families. Most of them brought their families who stayed in the camp where they were stationed.

One of the duties of the district advisors was to go out on a mission with the district's RF/PF units, particularly the District Intelligence Squad. Unlike other larger units, this squad only consisted of seven to ten professional and native soldiers. They knew the territory so well that they could roam around the jungle without a compass. The squad's primary objective was to collect intelligence on enemy movement and infiltrate suspected enemy base camps, a vital source of information for those units operating in the region. When they operated by themselves, they dressed as Viet Cong in black farmer's clothing with straw hats and armed themselves with AK-47 rifles. Of course, with the American advisors' presence on any operation, their disguise became useless.

One day I was with the District Intelligence Squad on a reconnaissance operation in coordination with the 7th Regiment Reconnaissance Company. The objective of the operation was a suspected NVA resupply base camp along the Song Be River east of Chon Thanh. The majority of the dense jungle in the district territory had been sprayed with chemical defoliant, but part of the terrain along the Song Be River was still covered with overgrown foliage. Hardly penetrable from aerial observation, it became an ideal sanctuary for NVA troop movement and for setting up NVA base camps. The first two days of the operation were calm and uneventful. In the afternoon of the third day, as our squad swept around the suspected NVA infiltration route, one of the reconnaissance company columns ran into an unknown size NVA element. After almost an hour-long fire fight, the enemy retreated leaving their food supply behind. We called for artillery to fire on the retreating enemy route. Then we continued to move toward the objective.

The next day, about noon, we reached Song Be River. At first it was quiet. As we made a quick sweep in an area under a heavy, shady canopy of bamboo trees, we discovered many camouflaged shallow shelters and storage sheds dotting the bank of the river that stretched nearly a mile long. Nevertheless, there was no enemy in sight. We also found a few bowls of freshly cooked rice, plates of fish and vegetables on a bamboo table, indicating only a few guards had been guarding the site. They must have fled in a hurry as we approached the camp. We decided to set some of the structures on fire and destroy the food supply as fast as possible, then retreated after we called in artillery fire on the camp.

One of the main challenges in remote villages was providing healthcare for the locals. They rarely had sufficient resources to care for their own health and, in most cases, they would not come to the clinic unless they were seriously ill or about to die. Subsequently, most of the cases in the clinic were either gravely serious or lost causes altogether. The only clinic in town was a single-story yellow building located outside the district compound. It had an office and two inpatient wards (for those who had to travel from remote villages for treatment). The clinic was primitive and frequently short of medical supplies. Mr. Nam, the only medical worker in town, was in charge of the whole operation. He worked so hard, but he could only do so much on his own. In order to improve the health condition of the villagers, the U.S. advisory team frequently set up mobile clinics in remote villages to treat the sick and wounded. In many cases we evacuated the seriously ill to hospitals where they received proper treatment.

Chon Thanh district covered about 160 square miles of flat terrain, more than two thirds of it was natural, dense forest. It stretched from QL-13 to Song Be River to the east and to Tay Ninh province to the west. The forest was the main source of income for the locals. Its teak and mahogany wood were suitable for construction and furniture. With such a heavy canopy of foliage, it became an ideal sanctuary and infiltration route for Viet Cong and NVA troops operating in the area.

U.S. airplanes began defoliant spray operations around Chon Thanh well before I arrived. The spray was applied from the air to remote areas, and by personnel around the perimeter of military fortifications and villages — even just a few yards away from houses of local residents. The defoliant was so effective that within days of spraying, the trees started shedding leaves and foliage that turned brown and died. Every time I flew over an affected area during air reconnaissance, I could easily spot everything on the ground. Obviously the defoliant spray served its purpose in denying the enemy a haven. However, no one realized at the time that the widely-used defoliant, also called Agent Orange, was a toxic chemical. By the time it was banned in 1971, the damage had been done. People exposed to this dioxin-laced chemical had an increased risk of cancer, birth defects, and many forms of skin diseases.

Over the years, many soldiers like me had been roaming the jungle to conduct combat operations in defoliated areas. We did not know that in addition to the real enemy we fought against in the jungle, there was another invisible foe. It was more deadly than the bullets and bombs. It lurked in the soil we trod, the air we breathed, and the water we drank from contaminated streams. More than four decades after U.S. forces withdrew from Vietnam, questions remain about the lasting health consequences. I have been blessed with excellent health in my years off the battlefield, but for many people who were more exposed to Agent Orange, the story is different.

In January, 1969, a young woman brought her son who was complaining of a swollen jaw to the small clinic in town. The nurse assumed he had a gum infection, gave him some antibiotics and sent him home. A month later, the nurse called me to the clinic. I was shocked to see this poor little four-year-old boy's deformed face. A grapefruit-sized tumor was embedded in his right jaw, the weight of it sank his head to one side. The swelling caused his right eye to be permanently shut. He tried to peek at me, as if hoping for a miracle cure. Obviously he was in tremendous pain and unable to eat, yet he did not cry. His mother begged me to do anything to find a cure for him. The clinic nurse suggested I take the boy to a larger hospital to get proper treatment. The next morning I took the boy to a hospital at the 2nd Field Force Headquarters in Long Binh for a biopsy. When the result came back, the boy was diagnosed with incurable, soft-tissue sarcoma (a type of cancer later confirmed to be caused by exposure to defoliant herbicides). There was no treatment available in Vietnam at that time.

I remember the afternoon I walked into the small, wood frame house where the boy and his family lived in Chon Thanh I village. I stood by his bedside and told his mother the terrible news. It was one of my toughest assignments. The boy was terribly sick, yet awake. His tumor now had grown much larger, pushing his mouth to one side. He could no longer talk except for a few mumbling words. At times, he rolled his head back and forth in agony. His mother sat by his bed caressing his hands and wept. She was desperate and refused to give up hope. The last resort was to take the boy to a Vietnamese cancer center in Phu Nhuan near Saigon for radiation treatment. The advisory team agreed to arrange transportation for the family and take care of the admission process. Two weeks later I received word that the little boy had passed away.

There were happy moments in our work with the Chon Thanh clinic. One evening in July 1969, I received a call from Mr. Nam asking for help. The team medic, Sgt. Smith, and I hurried to the clinic. Lying in the primitive inpatient ward was a 40-year-old pregnant, diabetic woman who was having seizures just as she was about to deliver the baby. We realized it was more than the clinic could handle. She needed to be evacuated to a hospital where she could receive proper care. We called for a medevac helicopter and then placed her in the back seat of a jeep. We rushed her to a dark, unsecured helicopter pad nearby. As I saw the helicopter approaching in the dark sky, the woman started to deliver her baby in the back seat of the jeep. We had no other choice but to radio the helicopter to stay back. I held a flashlight while Sgt. Smith used a pair of scissors to cut and tie the umbilical cord of the newborn baby boy. He wrapped the baby in a blanket and cleaned up the mother before the helicopter landed and took them away. A week later, the woman returned home with a 3.7 kilogram (8.15 lbs.), healthy boy. She thanked us for what we did. It was heartwarming to see the joy in the face of this new mother as she brought her adorable baby boy to her family.

Aside from the military effort to take control of villages and meet the needs of the local people, the advisory team was often involved in events beyond their responsibility. One afternoon, as Capt. Ralph Cruikshank (the district senior advisor who succeeded Capt. Gallagher) and I returned from a village visit, I received a call from the district Tactical Operations Center (TOC) that a fire had broken out at Chon Thanh II village on the north end of the town. The fire was spreading rapidly due to strong winds. Within minutes, five houses had been destroyed. We quickly mobilized a PF platoon and every American advisor available to help fight the fire. We used buckets to draw water from wells to douse the straw roof and side walls of the house to prevent the raging fire from spreading further. After two hours we were exhausted, but the fire was threatening to engulf the entire village. Finally, we called in a fire-fighting CH-47 Chinook helicopter from Lai Khe to put out the fire. When the smoke cleared, at least half of the houses in the village were saved. The next day the village chief paid a visit to the district compound. He thanked us for saving his village.

Two months later I was called for an award ceremony in the team mess hall. Capt. Ralph Cruikshank pinned an Army Commendation Medal on me for my efforts in saving the village. I was proud of my contribution. It was the first medal awarded to me by the U.S. military.

– CHAPTER 5 –

Collateral Damages

Nevertheless, of all the noble deeds we accomplished in this small region, there were downsides as well. One of the most horrible things was the collateral damage to the innocent civilians who were caught in the middle of the firefight. While the Vietnamese district apparatus and its advisory teams had tried everything they could to protect civilians, some U.S. units operating in the district constantly fired upon unarmed civilians without confirming their identity with the district. The people who suffered the most were the woodcutters who entered the jungle every day to earn their living. From time to time they fell victim to U.S. helicopter gunships that mistakenly identified them as Viet Cong. We finally gave instructions to the woodcutters that, when they entered the wood, they must wear light-colored clothing, and their trucks must bear a South Vietnamese flag on top of the cabin.

One late night in the spring of 1969 as I was just about to get ready for bed, I received a call that My Chanh hamlet, a small village five miles south of the district, was under fire from Fire Support Base (FSB) Thunder II north of Bau Bang. A few minutes later, another call came in that a house in the hamlet had caught fire and a family was trapped inside. We notified the FSB to suspend all firing and Capt. Gallagher and I rushed to the scene. As we approached, we saw that the house that was engulfed in flames and giving off thick, heavy smoke. The hamlet chief came over to meet us with the tragic news. A family of six had lost their lives in the house. Only the older son, who happened to be staying with his friend in another house, had escaped. Apparently when the family heard the gunfire, they all took cover in the bomb shelter in the house. The house caught fire and collapsed over the bomb shelter, trapping and burning alive everyone inside.

I stood helplessly in front of the incinerated house, staring at the pile of still-smoldering wood beams where the charred bodies of the parents and their four children were buried underneath. Around the corner there were a couple of village elders trying to comfort the lone survivor of the family as he wailed and pounded his fists on the ground. How could anyone endure such tragedy? Capt. Gallagher and I walked over to console him and assured him we would launch an investigation first thing in the morning. It was a small consolation, wholly inadequate to replace what this young man had lost — but it was all we could do.

The next morning we returned to the scene, and the U.S. Army battalion commander in charge of the FSB was already there to launch an investigation. He expressed his condolences to the family and asked me to begin the process of compensation for the loss. At the same time, the villagers helped remove the bodies from the bomb shelter. According to the preliminary investigation report, that evening the FSB guards allegedly received gun fire from the direction of the hamlet and returned fire with machine guns and grenade launchers, accidentally setting the straw house on fire.

My heart ached every time I saw tragedies like this. Yes, this was war, which by nature is cruel and evil. Mistakes had been made, tragedy happened, and innocent people died no matter how hard we tried to prevent it. However, other tragedies might not have been caused by human error. Atrocities such as the infamous My Lai massacre and a few other incidents I had witnessed were committed by American soldiers who acted either out of frustration, ignorance, or even just for fun. We were all losers when such tragedies happened.

One afternoon the district chief, Maj. Nguen Van Thanh, called me to his office. He was angry and distraught by the news that an unknown fixed-wing airplane had killed two brothers on QL-13 between north of downtown and the Tau-O bridge. Obviously only U.S. military airplanes were operating in the area that morning. I immediately accompanied Maj. Thanh to the scene. I was in shock at the unspeakable horror before my eyes. A headless body was lying on the shoulder of the road. Blood and chunks of skull spread out on a large area of the asphalt pavement. Further down in the ditch was another headless body next to a light green and white Honda scooter lying on its side. Immediately we sent an RF squad to clean up the scene and launched an investigation. According to witnesses, a low flying U.S. L19 reconnaissance airplane came from nowhere, hitting the two victims who were on their way to visit their family in Chon Thanh. Within a week, the division command headquarters in Lai Khe issued a report that a U.S. army pilot was charged for the killing. The report also indicated the pilot suffered from mental illness. He was less than a week from completing his tour of duty in Vietnam.

Despite all of the horrific incidents U.S. armed servicemen committed, no matter how painful, I still see them as isolated incidents carried out senselessly by a few unruly individuals. Rest assured, most American GIs I met were decent, well-disciplined young men who followed the military code of conduct. They had no desire to kill innocent people. The South Vietnamese, in general, are a resilient and understanding people. They believed the American forces were taking on a noble cause in helping them defend their freedom when they could not do it on their own. I saw this every time I visited villages with American advisors and troops, providing medical care and food supplies for the neediest, or helping them to improve their living conditions. They welcomed the Americans as honored guests into their homes for a cold drink or a sumptuous feast.

This was a far cry from some of the cruel treatment American servicemen and women encountered when they returned home. They were scorned for their service in Vietnam and depicted as "baby killers" by the liberal media. Such anti-war rhetoric distorted the truth, and insulted noble servicemen and women and all freedom-loving people. I spent six years fighting on the battlefield, shoulder-to-shoulder with both American and South Vietnamese forces, and I can say with certainty that the media's portrayal of U.S. soldiers in Vietnam at that time was unfair, to say the least. To this day, I highly respect those who served in Vietnam, especially those who sacrificed their lives for the freedom of complete strangers on the other side of the world.

Despite some setbacks, in the early 1970s I began to see things turning around in this small town. Enemy attacks on or near the population center and the district compound had been steadily decreasing. Each week the district received, on average, twenty defectors from VC and NVA ranks to the district headquarters. They asked for asylum, and I had many opportunities to interview them. Among them were high-ranking NVA officers and VC cadres and family members of local prominent VC officials. It was a good sign because I never saw something like this in my three short years stationed in Chon Thanh. People no longer lived under constant fear of enemy attack and business in the town marketplace was booming. New housing projects popped up in every village and many villagers started repairing their run-down houses, expanding their farm land, and building more charcoal kilns. Woodcutters now had less fear of going into the woods. They purchased new equipment and trucks to transport lumber to customers in other parts of the country. Could peace finally arrive in this war torn country?

Looking back, peace in this part of the world at that point in time was merely a mirage, a glimmer of false hope. After being immersed for the first time in the cruelty of war, I still crossed my fingers in the hope that peace would eventually come true.

One late night in May 1970, I was getting ready for bed after a long day of travel and catching up on translation work when an explosion shook the barracks where I stayed.

"Incoming!" someone yelled, as more shells hit the center of the compound and bursts of machine gun fire pierced through the quiet night.

I grabbed my helmet and rifle and rushed to my designated defensive bunker along the barbed wire fence. Soon illumination flares lit up the moonless sky. Mortars exploded around me. The gunfire grew to a deafening roar.

"Tinh, VC's in the wire!" Sgt. Murphy, the team NCO, yelled as he rushed into my bunker. He carried an M60 machine gun. I looked through the porthole, and under the flickering of the flare lights, I saw several dark figures crawling under the outer layer of concertina wire. I fired my M16, emptying my first clip. I looked again as I reloaded my rifle. There was no more movement, only dust settling in the air.

I left my position to Sgt. Murphy and ran to the Tactical Operation Center (TOC) at the center of the compound. As I approached it in the dark, I stumbled into a crumbled sandbag wall at the entrance. The semi-underground bunker was hit by several incoming rounds. A mortar round struck the galvanized tin roof and shattered it to pieces. I found my way around and went into the TOC. Surprisingly, no one inside was hurt, most likely thanks to layers of sandbags on top of the roof that had absorbed many direct hits. Outside the bunker, one wall of the district office building had collapsed. The watchtower behind the advisory team barracks also got hit. Two PF soldiers, who were manning a machine gun on that tower, were seriously wounded. We sent medics to bring them down. Several fortified structures along the outer perimeter were damaged by B40 rockets. A few defenders suffered light wounds. Sgt. Tran Van Tan was guarding the bunker at the northwest corner of the compound when the attack started. As he looked through the porthole, he saw a VC dressed in black standing directly in front of the porthole. He fired his rifle. Then he saw the poor guy fall to the ground in front of the bunker.

Listening to the radio chatter, I realized the district was not the only place under attack. The 7th ARVN Regiment Compound located south of us, also was hit hard, and the enemy had infiltrated their defensive positions. The U.S. fire support base north of Chon Thanh also got hit by incoming rounds. The generator station near the market place in downtown Chon Tanh suffered damages by several B40 rockets. The 155mm howitzers stationed at other fire support bases started to shell suspected enemy locations. A large scale attack was underway. The attack and counterattack lasted until dawn.

As the sun rose, the enemy retreated, and everyone emerged from the defensive positions. As we ventured across the battlefield, we found that the district had suffered fifteen wounded. The 7th ARVN Regiment Compound had two of their men killed in action and more than twenty wounded. The enemy had left behind forty-two bodies. Documents found on the dead indicated they were elements of the 5th VC Division. Many bloody trails left at the scene also indicated they carried with them an unknown number of wounded as they retreated. Most of the dead were in the vicinity of the airstrip. It was likely they were caught in the open as they attacked the 7th ARVN Regiment Compound. There were also civilian casualties during the nighttime attack — the NVA fired two mortar rounds into the residential area killing two and wounding a dozen. No one knew whether this was intentional or just some stray shells.

In September, 1970, I received orders to be transferred to the Provincial Headquarters at An Loc to serve as the interpreter for the Province Senior Advisor. For me, the transfer was bittersweet. My new assignment involved mostly office work. Many considered it a promotion as now I could sit in the comfort of an air-conditioned office, working normal office hours. But in my new assignment I missed the bond of the local soldiers with whom I had fought side-by-side, the joy of helping to ease the pain of the villagers, and the satisfaction of seeing normalcy gradually come to people whose lives had been shattered by the war.

CHAPTER 6

Calm Before the Storm

It was almost noon April 4, 1972. The bus inched its way to the curb while people on foot and bicycles parted around it like water around a rock. The stench of exhaust mixed with sweat was suffocating on this hot and humid day, but by the end of the hour-long bus ride I barely noticed it. It had been a long journey from Saigon to An Loc. It was made even longer when the bus was stranded by mechanical problems. The passengers turned their weary, glistening faces toward the window looking for a familiar sign that this was their stop, but turned away, disappointed, when it was not. Across the street, the endless brick wall stacked with rows of concertina wires was a clue that a military complex was on the other side. All eyes looked to me. Yes, this was my stop, and I was grateful to get off.

I shouldered my duffel bag and waded through the constant stream of bicycles and automobiles until I had crossed the busy street. I went through the side gate of the main entrance as armed guards waved me in to the walled complex of Binh Long Provincial Administrative Headquarters.

I quickly passed the two-story, beige colonial building on my right where the Province Chief Col. Tran Van Nhut's office was located. A military jeep sat idly under the shade of the white canopy in the driveway. There was no one there. His driver and body guards had gone for lunch, I guessed. I headed toward the office of Military Advisory Team 47 at the far southwest corner of the complex. It was a medium-sized, one story building with glass-paned windows and green shutters. The Military Assistance Command and Civil Operations and Rural Development Support (MACCORDS) building housed MACV military advisors, as well as the CORDS civilian personnel.

I pushed opened the half-glass wooden front door. A blast of air-conditioned air snapped me out of the stupor left over from the hot and wearisome journey.

"Hi Sgt. Tinh, so glad to see you're back." Miss Huong, the office clerk, halted her typing to greet me. "Lt. Col. Corley looked for you this morning."

"Thanks. It's good to be back again." I wasted no time as I walked past her desk and headed toward the Senior Advisor's office.

Lt. Col. Robert Corley was the Province Senior Advisor, a U.S. Army Corps of Engineers officer before taking command of the advisory team. He was the third Province Senior Advisor I served during my stay in An Loc.

"Good morning sir! Sorry I'm late," I said as I pushed open the swinging door of his office.

"Sgt. Tinh, I want you to go with Maj. Davidson to Loc Ninh," he said slowly rising from his chair, flicking open his lighter to light his cigar. "Something very urgent has come up. I know you've worked with Maj. Davidson before. I need you go with him to Loc Ninh for an emergency meeting with the staff of the 9th Infantry Regiment. The 5th Infantry Division commander Lt. Gen. Le Van Hung will preside over the meeting. His advisor also will be there. The meeting is at 1300h. You don't have much time, so go get your stuff and meet Maj. Davidson immediately."

"Yes sir, I'm going right away" I answered and left without any further questions.

I had been translating intelligence reports since 1967 in this region and as far as I could tell in the past couple of years, the North Vietnamese war effort in Binh Long Province was winding down. More and more Viet Cong and NVA soldiers were deserting to the Republic of Vietnam every week. Locals were moving about freely and conducting business without fear of Viet Cong extortion or NVA military attack. When I left for Saigon the previous week, the Binh Long Province was relatively calm. But now, all that had changed.

The U.S. and South Vietnam intelligence apparatus had recently received reports detailing increased NVA activities along the Vietnam/Cambodia border. All signs pointed to a massive enemy buildup for a possible major attack on Tay Ninh province (west of Binh Long) within several days. Maj. Davidson represented the 47th Military Advisory Team at the intelligence briefing with Lt. Gen. Hung, the commanding general of the 5th ARVN Division, at the 9th Regiment Headquarters at Loc Ninh. I was to be Maj. Davidson's interpreter.

I called Maj. Davidson and arranged to meet him at the officer barracks. I went to my apartment, put on my uniform, picked up my M16 rifle and gear and walked over to the officer barracks. By the time I arrived, Maj. Davidson had packed everything in his jeep and was waiting for me.

"Ready to go, Sgt. Tinh?" he asked.

"Yes, let's go!" I replied as I threw my backpack in the back seat. Maj. Davidson walked around to the driver's side of the jeep. On his way there, he stopped short and cursed.

"G---damn flat" he growled, kicking the deflated front tire in frustration. Now we were late for the meeting.

The first time I met Maj. Thomas A. (Drew) Davidson was during my assignment in Chon Thanh district three months before. As the drawdown of U.S. military forces was ending, the U.S. military advisors at the district level were phasing out and turning the military operations to the Vietnamese forces. At that time, Maj. Davidson was the only U.S. advisor in the district and was in need of an interpreter who was familiar with the territory. Since I had served in Chon Thanh for more than three years, I was an excellent fit for the assignment.

Maj. Davidson, a native of Lewisburg, Tennessee, served two tours of duty in Vietnam as a Bird Dog (reconnaissance) pilot. At the drawdown of U.S. combat units, he signed up for another tour as a military advisor to Advisory Team 47. Unlike any other advisors I had worked with, Maj. Davidson was an outspoken guy, yet easygoing and never discriminating against others. He built a strong relationship with his Vietnamese counterparts, Lt. Col. Pham Quang My and the district staff. However, his outspoken manner sometimes irked Lt. Col. Robert Corley.

When the U.S. advisory team finally pulled out from Chon Thanh as scheduled, Maj. Davidson was reassigned to S3 (Military Operation) in An Loc, and I returned to my previous post as interpreter for Lt. Col. Corley. I took a week off before reporting for duty.

We fixed the flat and headed north on QL-13. This stretch of QL-13, from An Loc to the border of Cambodia, was a two-lane, red dirt road about twenty feet wide. Despite the fact that ARVN minesweepers cleared the road every morning, no matter what time we traveled down QL-13 was at our own risk. The enemy would frequently lay mines on the side of the road at night and ambush convoys in broad daylight. The best way to avoid triggering a land mine was to drive down the middle of the two-lane road, avoiding the shoulders as much as possible. This, unfortunately, was complicated by potholes and bombed-out craters that dotted most of the length of the road. The Army Engineer Corps was stretched thin trying to make the road minimally drivable. Even doing the road repairs was risky — often they would be shot at, without warning, from the tree line.

As the jeep nimbly weaved down the road leaving a trail of swirling red dust behind, I tightened my finger around the trigger of my M16, carefully watching for anything resembling the telltale flash of an RPG40 rocket fired from the tree line. The battle lines of this war zone were hazy at best — no place was ever truly safe.

As we approached Thien Phat Hamlet, more than halfway between An Loc and Loc Ninh, I saw several buses overloaded with villagers traveling south, their luggage and furniture strapped precariously to the top of the bus. The caravan of buses ambled down the road, tilting side to side in what looked like a drunken stupor.

"It looks like they're getting out of town, *Thieu Ta* (Major)," I said, pointing to the buses.

"Well, someone must have told them the VC are coming," Maj. Davidson replied as he swerved to avoid another pot hole. "If the situation is as bad as that report says it is, they're the smarter ones."

"So what does that make us?" I asked, mostly to myself, as a cloud of red dust kicked up by the passing buses engulfed the jeep.

"Tinh, if what we know is true, we may not come back alive."

Given the situation we were in, I knew he was not joking at all.

We arrived at Loc Ninh's town square at two in the afternoon. Loc Ninh, 20 miles north of An Loc, was a prosperous plantation town, and most of its 2,000 residents worked for the French-owned Cexso Rubber Plantation. Its rubber trees stood in row upon row, stretching for miles across the hills from the south through the town toward the Cambodian border.

The jeep turned left onto a red dirt road leading to the town's only airstrip, passing the red-roofed colonial villas owned by the French plantation managers. The green lawn, beautiful tropical flower gardens, huge-sized swimming pool, and tennis court stood in stark contrast to the rusted, tin-roof houses down the hill and the rustic district compound a few hundred yards to the south. The plantation managers were "neutral" in this war. On one hand, they invited the local government officials and the U.S. and South Vietnamese military officers to dine at their luxurious villas, but on the other hand, they paid "protection fees" to the NVA, so they would not damage their property and rubber trees.

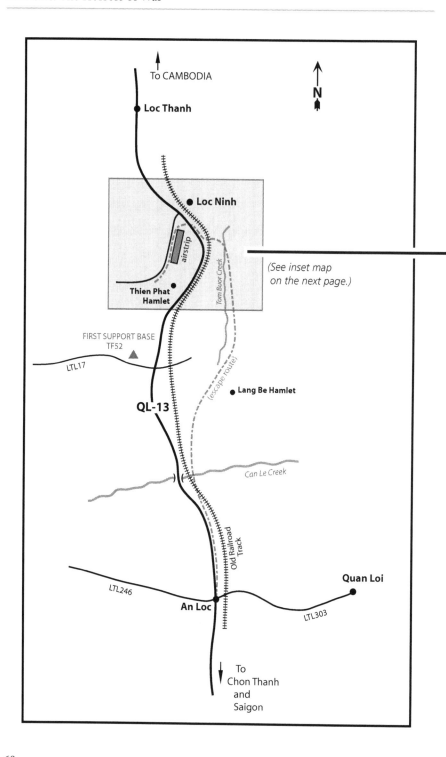

To CAMBODIA

N

● Loc Thanh

● Loc Ninh

airstrip

Tom Buor Creek

Thien Phat
Hamlet
●

(See inset map
on the next page.)

FIRST SUPPORT BASE
TF52 ▲

LTL17

(escape route)

QL-13

● Lang Be Hamlet

Can Le Creek

Old Railroad Track

Quan Loi ●

LTL246

An Loc ●

LTL303

To
Chon Thanh
and
Saigon

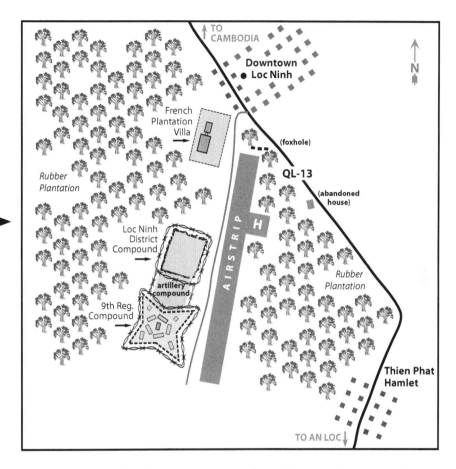

We arrived at the district compound on the west side of the airstrip. The compound was ringed by three rows of concertina wires stacked two high with barbed wire fence in between. Behind the fences were the outer bunkers fortified with wood beams, earthwork, and layers of sandbags on top. There was a fortified guard tower at each corner of the compound. At the center of the compound, there was the Tactical Operations Center (TOC), crowned with several 15-foot-tall radio antennas. Standing next to it was the camouflaged observation tower, encircled with offices and living quarters for the district chief, his staff and the American advisors. The outer fortified bunkers also served as living quarters for the Regional Force (RF) soldiers who defended the compound and their family dependents. Adjacent to the south along the air strip was the 9th ARVN Regiment Headquarters and an artillery compound.

As we pulled into the district compound, Capt. George K. Wanat Jr., Assistant District Senior Advisor, was waiting impatiently outside of his bunker to greet us. He hopped in the jeep and we headed for the 9th Regimental Compound.

Capt. Wanat was from Waterford, Connecticut. This was his first tour of duty in Vietnam. He was a thin, tall, soft-spoken gentleman. He was excited that the very next day would be his last day in Loc Ninh. Once his boss, Maj. Robert Blair (the District Senior Advisor) returned from R&R (rest and recuperation) in Bangkok, he would fly to An Loc and return to the United States for good, subsequently ending his tour.

We parked the jeep outside the conference room. Maj. Davidson told me to stay outside since the meeting was already in progress. He said there was no need to disrupt the meeting. He would get all the details afterward.

I looked around. There was nothing in sight to shade me from the scorching, hot sun. I brushed off the red dust clinging to my green uniform and sat down on the driver's side of the jeep. As I flipped through the pages of a newspaper I had brought along, I heard a commotion from the conference room. It consisted, for the most part, of Lt. Gen. Hung furiously berated Col. Nguyen Cong Vinh, the 9th Regimental Commander, for his lack of response to the intelligence they had collected. It later became clear that Col. Vinh had no intention to put up a fight with NVA at the onset of the enemy attack. In the end, many lives were lost because of his cowardice and subsequent surrender to the enemy.

As I tried to eavesdrop on the verbal lashing emanating from the conference room, someone came from behind and stood next to me.

"Hello, my name is Michel, Michel Dumond." He spoke with a French accent, a black camera hanging over his chest.

"Sgt. Tinh," I reached out to shake his hand. "I'm from An Loc. You must be a reporter?"

"Yes, I just came from Lai Khe this morning with Capt. (Mark) Smith."

"There must be something going on to bring you all the way to Loc Ninh." I was curious.

"Well, I don't know yet, it could be something big," he replied.

We chatted for a while. Then he returned to his bunker.

The meeting ended after four in the afternoon. Lt. Gen. Hung and his advisor, Col. William H. Miller, came out of the meeting room, boarded their helicopter and returned to the division headquarters in Lai Khe.

We returned to the district compound. It was already past four o'clock, and the road to An Loc had been closed and unsafe to travel. We had no other option but to stay overnight. That evening Maj. Davidson and I went to a Vietnamese cafeteria inside the compound to have a bowl of Vietnamese noodle soup. The soup was hot and salty with too much *nuoc-mam* (fish sauce) in it. I was just happy to have something to fill my grumbling stomach. I had not had any food since breakfast that morning.

That evening I returned to the district TOC. I received a report that the 9th Reconnaissance Company of 70 men from the 9th ARVN Regiment was wiped out by a large NVA unit just west of Loc Ninh. A wounded radio operator was the lone survivor of the onslaught. Further reports indicated that within the last two weeks, three NVA divisions and supporting elements (about 35,000 men strong) had left their base camps in the Snoul area inside Cambodia bordering Loc Ninh. Initially, the intelligence analysts at Military Region 3 Headquarters in Bien Hoa speculated that Tay Ninh province to the west was the likely target giving the recent history of enemy attacks. However, intelligence received that morning indicated the NVA divisions had moved toward An Loc and Loc Ninh.

Early that morning, a Regional Force (RF) unit, under the command of the district chief operating west of the Loc Ninh area, discovered communication wires strung across a wide area. Also, there were many track prints of NVA T54 tanks left in the woods — a telltale sign of the presence of a large enemy force in the area. This alarming news was unprecedented. Since the beginning of the Vietnam War, neither the NVA nor their Viet Cong insurgents in the South dared to launch a conventional offensive in division-sized force to challenge the overpowering U.S. military might, even with a force complemented with mechanized units. Now that the U.S. military had withdrawn much of its ground troops, a looming battle was taking shape. The NVA was going to launch a major offensive before the start of the monsoon season which would arrive the end of May. It was not a matter of when, but where.

I stayed in Mr. Nguyen Van Tuong's bunker that night. Mr. Tuong was a civilian interpreter working for Maj. Blair. A native of Hanoi, Tuong fled south with his parents in 1955 and resettled in Saigon. Though he was exempted from military service for disability reasons, he liked the lucrative pay he received from serving in this high risk area. I told him he should find another job in Saigon where he could stay closer to his family. He insisted he needed the money to support his parents and his younger siblings.

I was so tired and yet did not know how I drifted off to sleep. That night the faint sound of constant explosions from afar had no effect on me at all. The battle had arrived at our doorstep, and it was the last good night's rest I would have for a long time.

– CHAPTER 7 –

The Battle of Loc Ninh

It was early in the morning April 5, 1972. A huge explosion shook me out of bed. I grabbed my rifle and helmet and quickly slipped on my boots. I rushed to the underground bunker entrance as Mr. Tuong came running down the stairs.

"Tinh, we are under attack, you'd better go right to the TOC — they need you there." The frantic look on his face was clear. This was it.

I ran outside and saw Maj. Davidson and Capt. Wanat dashing out of the TOC carrying a radio. A barrage of rockets and mortar rounds exploded and I dropped to the ground as debris rained down on me.

"Go over to the command bunker!" Maj. Davidson yelled.

"Where is it?" I yelled back as I got up again. I did not know what he was talking about.

"Follow me!" he replied.

I ran across the narrow field in front of the TOC and joined them as more incoming rockets exploded. We took cover behind a six-foot-high Z-shaped sandbag wall that protected the entrance of the bunker until there was a lull in the barrage. We passed through a thick wooden door, making a U-turn into a pitch dark stairway. The air smelled moldy and damp. Someone flicked open a cigarette lighter to lead the way. We hurried down a flight of 40 stairs into a 30-by-20-foot room with a vaulted ceiling. Two bare bulbs dangled on a piece of wire in the center of the room. The only furniture was a small wooden desk and a bench placed near a corner with some dusty radio equipment stacked on top. The brown mud floor was dry and uneven.

I had heard about this legendary, well-fortified bunker for quite some time, yet this was the first time I had ever set foot inside. It was the safest place to stay should the enemy attack Loc Ninh. During World War II the Japanese Army built this underground bunker. Since it was more than 20 feet underground it could easily withstand a direct hit, even from the impact of a 500 lb. bomb. The bunker had four camouflaged entrances located at four corners of the compound. I recalled that on October 29, 1967, (while I was stationed at Chon Thanh District) the compound was under attack by a regiment-sized NVA force. The enemy punched through the outer perimeter and threw satchel charges from bunker to bunker to kill everyone inside. The former district chief, Capt. Tran Minh Cong, and ten of his men hunkered down inside the fortified underground bunker. When the defenders ran out of ammunition they called on artillery and air strikes. They were dropping bombs on top of the bunker as the enemy threw satchel charges and grenades from the top of the stairways. By the time the enemy retreated the next morning, the defenders emerged from the bunker with no casualties. However, the enemy left behind more than 200 dead comrades in the compound and on the nearby runway.

Capt. Wanat immediately set up the radio, connecting to a cable that led to an external antenna. Maj. Nguyen Van Thinh, District Chief of Loc Ninh, and his TOC staff finally came in with their communication equipment. Maj. Thinh was only five feet tall and was well-known by his peers as a womanizer. He was a former ARVN Ranger company commander before taking the helm as district chief of this small rubber plantation town. His cheerful reputation notwithstanding, his face was now set in stone as he barked orders to those of us in the room and those on the outer perimeter. A twinge of fear laced each of his commands.

The first thing he did was order the 225th Regional Force company operating near the Loc Ninh town square to retreat to the district compound to strengthen the 100-plus defenders, leaving five policemen and one policewoman to guard the police station in the town square.

The 9th ARVN Regiment compound and the artillery compound to the south were hit hard. Further south, the NVA simultaneously launched massive mortar and rocket attacks on Fire Support Base TF52 which was located near the junction of QL-13 and LTL-17. Quan Loi Base, east of downtown An Loc, and the Chon Thanh District Compound, were also under attack. Lt. Col. Pham Quang My, the Chon Thanh district chief who Maj. Davison and I once worked with, was wounded. His bodyguard was killed instantly when an enemy rocket slammed into his living quarters.

We were doomed from the moment the attack started. How could we defend this small compound with only 200-plus RF and PF soldiers? How were we supposed to fight against more than 35,000 NVA soldiers? Later reports indicated the 9th VC Division, 7th NVA Division and other elements bypassed Loc Ninh to move south toward An Loc, setting the stage of attack on the provincial capital once they took control of Loc Ninh. Only the 5th VC Division, joined by the 272nd and 273rd Regiments, an artillery regiment and an anti-aircraft gun battery, were left to take part in the offensive in Loc Ninh.

All day long the NVA pounded the district compound with rockets, artillery and mortar rounds. In the afternoon we saw movement in the rubber plantation on the west and the east side across the airstrip. We called in air strikes on these suspected targets. Soon the NVA used loudspeakers to announce they had us all surrounded and demanded us to surrender before they launched ground attack. We had heard it all before — NVA propaganda was nothing new — and we called for more air strikes on their positions.

Late in the afternoon a report came from the pilot of a Forward Air Control (FAC) aircraft stationed over the area. He had spotted several enemy trucks possibly towing large pieces of artillery guns toward the downtown bus station. He asked for permission to destroy the trucks. Maj. Thinh asked the pilot to make a few passes to verify the color of the truck and the equipment they carried. Minutes later, they reported the suspected trucks belonged to civilian loggers hauling logs from the forest. We breathed a sigh of relief.

As night fell, the bombing intensified. During the night the NVA launched massive ground attacks with tank support from the plantation to the west and across the air strip from the east. The defenders fought desperately, and were only able to repulse the attacks with the support of two AC130 Spectre gunships and bombers dropping Cluster Bomb Unit (CBU) and napalm bombs. We also suffered heavy casualties. Lt. Quang, the one and only army surgeon in the compound, reported that his tiny dispensary had become so overcrowded with wounded soldiers and civilians that he had to expand to the cafeteria next door. There was no place for the dead. He stacked the bodies on the ground outside the dispensary.

By midnight the soldiers from the observation tower at the top of the command bunker reported there were mortar rounds firing from the drained swimming pool in the French plantation villa. There was also a mysterious light on the second floor of the building. Every time the light was turned off, mortars and rockets started raining down on us. Obviously the NVA was using the second floor of the villa as an observation post. Maj. Davidson requested permission to destroy the villa. However, for some unknown reason, the ARVN headquarters denied the request. We kept pleading to no avail. Finally, Maj. Thinh and Maj. Davidson decided to destroy the villa in spite of the headquarters' rejection. Maj. Thinh ordered his men to fire 106mm recoilless launchers and Maj. Davidson called for air strikes on the villa.

We had no idea who fired the shot to destroy the villa. All we knew was that within minutes, the villa was engulfed in flames and then crumbled. The intensity of the shelling from the villa had reduced dramatically.

The next morning, April 6, the ground attack subsided. Though sporadic rockets and mortars were still hitting the compound, Maj. Davidson and I decided to go outside the bunker to survey the damage. As we walked past the outer perimeter, we saw the devastation just one day of fighting had caused. Some bunkers had collapsed and dead bodies were lying on top or buried inside. Dead enemy soldiers were still tangled in the barbed wire and scattered along the airstrip outside the compound. No one bothered to remove them. Most of the buildings above ground in the center had been destroyed. A few RF soldiers were taking advantage of the lull to mend the battered bunkers while others prepared lunch. They were weary and tired. They did not bother to look at us as we waved at them.

Maj. Davidson decided to go to the outdoor latrine, while I returned to the bunker. A few minutes later, Maj. Davidson returned looking slightly shaken. He was nearly killed by a mortar round that struck the roof of the latrine just as he was walking away from it.

After more than a day of dreadful fighting, the promised reinforcements were nowhere to be seen. Reports that morning indicated Lt. Gen. Hung had ordered the 252nd battalion task force to mount a counterattack to reinforce the besieged Loc Ninh compounds. However, they immediately ran into an ambush near the junction of QL-13 and LTL-17 and retreated to their camp. Mobilizing any reinforcement from any other part of the region could take at least one more day. Given the wide scale of attacks, our hope for outside help faded. The only hope was to rely heavily on air supports or that the enemy might soon give up and retreat.

By mid-morning, the generator that supplied power to the command bunker was dead. No one bothered to check it out. It was most likely damaged by the enemy fire. We lit the room with a kerosene lamp. It was barely bright enough to illuminate the corner where all the radio equipment was. The C-ration meals could not last for another day and we were nearly out of drinking water. The situation in the room was getting desperate. No one knew how we could feed the 30 people who were in the bunker.

In order to raise the morale of the troops, Maj. Thinh allowed some of the defenders' dependents to take shelter in the command bunker, but there was no more room for them except along the stairways.

The situation for the adjacent 9th Regiment compound was much worse than I thought. Capt. Mark "Zippo" Smith, a seasoned veteran on his fifth tour in Vietnam who spoke fluent Vietnamese, had taken over the command of the battle. At first we were all confused with the decision. Information surfaced throughout the day indicating Col. Nguyen Cong Vinh, the commander of the 9th ARVN Infantry regiment, was so shaken by the intensity of the attack that he had already prepared to surrender. He relinquished his command and Capt. Smith fully took over the battlefield.

Now every fire support request for the battle had to go through Capt. Smith, including any support for us in the district compound. As the fighting continued, tension mounted. Maj. Davidson was upset because of the delays each time he requested air strike on enemy positions or to fend off enemy attacks. They got into arguments and accusations during the height of the fighting.

Before noon, the defenders on the east side of the perimeter reported that a band of NVA soldiers were forcing a group of civilian women and children carrying an American flag to march from the town square toward the compounds. The civilians fled back to town only after the district compound defenders fired warning shots to disperse them.

More grim news came in the afternoon. We lost radio contact with the police station in the town square. The five brave policemen and one policewoman had been under attack since yesterday, and presumably were overrun by the NVA. The casualties were unknown.

By late afternoon, the NVA launched a ground attack with tank support from the east and west sides. The tanks penetrated the perimeter only to be driven back by air strikes, but we suffered more losses. The situation was deteriorating rapidly. Lt. Quang, the district surgeon, was killed when a rocket slammed into his overcrowded dispensary while he was treating the wounded.

Soon after this, a group of RF soldiers defending the outer perimeter started retreating to the command bunker. They were all shaken up by the intensity of the attack; their faces covered with dirt and blood. Capt. Wanat saw the situation, and he and I walked over to talk to Maj. Thinh.

"Sir, what is going on with these people here?" Capt. Wanat pointed to the group standing near the stairway.

"They are all scared! They don't want to be out there anymore," Maj. Thinh replied.

"But we need them to defend the perimeter. Can you order them out before the NVA swarm the place?"

"I can't. They need someone to lead them and their platoon leader has been killed," Maj. Thinh said, trying to find an excuse.

"You must appoint someone to take his place or, better yet, you go out with them," Capt. Wanat was not happy with the answer.

"No, I don't have anyone else," he insisted.

Capt. Wanat was infuriated. He pulled out his pistol and pointed it at Maj. Thinh's face.

"I'll blow your f--ing head off if you don't get these guys out of the g--damn bunker right now!" He barked at him in frustration, startling everyone in the bunker.

Finally, Maj. Thinh backed off. He instructed that anyone who could walk must leave the bunker and return to defend the compound. At least twenty men left the room and reluctantly returned to their defensive positions. They knew their chances of surviving the next phase of the enemy attack were slim, but what choice did they have? At one point, I considered going out and fighting alongside them. However, the truth of the matter was that I must stay to coordinate the air strikes. I could use my radio much better than my M16 to fend off the enemy.

Though the situation in the bunker had calmed down after Capt. Wanat's tirade, the air was still filled with tension as we came to grips with reality. How long could we hold out without any reinforcements? Unless the enemy withdrew, air strikes alone would not be enough to prevent them from overrunning the compound. As night fell for the second day of the siege, our hopes for rescue grew more dim.

By nightfall, an NVA sapper unit punched through the perimeter again. They reached the center of the compound and entered the dispensary, firing randomly at every wounded patient still alive, even those already dead could not escape a second slaughter. Again, they were driven out by a Spectre gunship. By now, there were fewer than 30 soldiers left to defend the outer perimeter. The wounded had no place to go except the command bunker. Two of the wounded soldiers died overnight. Someone covered the dead with a blanket and left them at the stairway. At midnight, another wave of ground attackers came in from the east, and again there were more wounded crammed into the already crowded bunker. We ran out of first aid kits, not even a bandage to dress their wounds. Their groans and moans added to the already miserable surroundings.

We were hungry, sleepless and dead tired. Hope of outside help now had totally vanished. All we were waiting for was the enemy's final assault.

The next morning, April 7, was eerily quiet. A few, sparse rocket and mortar rounds landed inside the already crumbled compound. Was it the calm before the final assault? At about eight o'clock in the morning, the soldier manning the observation tower reported that he saw a white flag raised on the flag pole inside the 9th Regiment compound. Also, there were many soldiers taking off their uniforms and walking out of their bunkers, their hands held high with white T-shirts. As they marched on the air strip passing the district compound, they were mowed down by NVA fire from the plantation across from the air strip. A few minutes later he reported that the white flag disappeared from the flag pole. What was going on? Could it be that the whole regiment surrendered? What about the U.S. advisors stationed there? We were trying to figure out what was going on, but there was no one to give us an answer.

Interestingly enough, there was no one in the command bunker who even mentioned surrendering. Perhaps it was because most of us were junior soldiers, except Maj. Thinh and four of his staff. We all understood well how we would be treated if the NVA captured us. They would interrogate ARVN officers for intelligence and hold U.S. military personnel as bargaining chips and for propaganda purposes. As for most of the junior ARVN soldiers like me, there was not much difference between surrendering and being killed by enemy fire. As an army interpreter, they would consider me a traitor because I worked with the Americans. I would most likely be executed.

A little after nine o'clock that morning, soldiers on the east side bunker line reported at least ten enemy tanks heading north on the airstrip. Some of them crashed through the 9th ARVN compound gate. Two others headed toward the district compound. They crashed through the barbed wire fences and fired on the defensive positions. At the same time, a large group of NVA punched through defensive lines from the northeast and west. However, the pilot of the Forward

Air Control (FAC) aircraft station over the area that morning could not identify our exact position because of the overcast sky in the entire region. He instructed us to run the engine of a vehicle so he might be able to locate our position with the sensing equipment on board.

"I'm going to start the engine of my jeep right now!" Mr. Tuong, (Maj. Blair's interpreter) volunteered. He sped up the stairway. A few minutes later he returned shaking his head and trying to catch his breath.

"I got my jeep running, but it was like hell up there. I don't know how long we can hold on!"

"Did you see any enemy?" I asked.

"No, but they are definitely inside the compound."

We waited for the air strike, but it never came. Later, I was told that B52 bombers were just about to make a bombing run on the plantation to the west and all other aircraft had to clear out of the way. During this critical moment, the enemy swamped our defensive positions forcing less than ten of the remaining defenders to retreat to the command bunker, including the one from the observation tower. Then the NVA soldiers threw satchel charges and grenades into any bunkers they could find, including the camouflaged entrances of the command bunker. Several hand grenades rolled down two of the stairways, exploded halfway in and killed more than 10 soldiers. We held our breath, turned down our radio and dimmed the only kerosene light in the room. We waited for the moment of death to come. At one side of the dark wall, a few mothers covered their children's mouths with their hands. They were afraid anyone crying might give away our location in the bunker.

Half an hour had gone by. There was no enemy movement at any entrance. Perhaps they assumed a couple of grenades thrown down the stairways would be enough to finish or flush out the defenders. A small fire, caused by hand grenades, broke out in one of the stairways and was immediately put out.

– CHAPTER 8 –

Trapped Underground

Now we were totally trapped and surrounded. The mood in the bunker was tense. It was deathly quiet. Over in the dark corner across from where I sat, a few children and their mothers choked up and sobbed quietly. We were all scared. I sensed death now standing in the doorway waiting to snatch each one of us. A chill ran up my spine. It was dark, and the smell of the room was strangely damp like the odor of death inside a tomb. Capt. Tam, the S3 officer, took out his rosary and whispered prayers as his radio crackled in the background.

Maj. Thinh came over and pulled out his shiny .38 pistol.

"Tinh, I have a total of five bullets, three of them for the VC's and two for myself." He showed me his only weapon. His hands were shaking and his voice trembled. "I was born in North (Vietnam) and I would rather take my own life than be captured. But before I kill myself, I'm going to take some of them with me." He tried to control himself and not show any sign of resignation.

Capt. Wanat was on the radio trying to contact the advisory team headquarters in An Loc for further instructions. Maj. Gen. James Hollingsworth, commander of the Third Regional Assistance Command (TRAC), constantly monitored the situation from his helicopter high over the battlefield, and kept assuring his advisors trapped underground that he was trying everything in his power to rescue them.

Maj. Davidson and I sat quietly on the cold, filthy dirt floor next to the radio. Given the dire situation we were in, we had done everything we could. I had not given up any hope of rescue; yet it would take more than a miracle to get out of this place alive. I leaned against the wall next to the doorway, thinking about my parents, siblings and friends. I could imagine the grief they would suffer, especially my mother. There was not much I could do but pray.

"Oh Lord! I'm crying out to you from the depth of the grave, mired in darkness. Rescue me from the hand of my enemy and be with me as you have promised." I almost burst into tears.

I opened my eyes. The room was still the same: dark and eerily quiet. Could God rescue me from this awful, hopeless situation?

It was three in the afternoon. The constant air strikes seemed to be holding the enemy at bay. Strangely, more than five hours had gone by and the enemy had not yet discovered the underground bunker. We held our breath. Even in this hopeless situation, we still hoped for the impossible.

Suddenly, a man's voice with a North Vietnamese dialect echoed from the top of the north entrance.

"Are there any Americans in here?"

"Yes, there are two of them," someone answered.

"You are all POWs now. I'll come back to get you."

I turned to Maj. Davidson. "Thieu Ta, we are sold out. Now the VC knows we are in here."

Maj. Davidson immediately got up with his M16 rifle in hand. He raced up the stairs and shot that man dead at the top of the stairway. Everyone was shocked, staring at him as he walked down the stairs.

"I'm not a f--ing POW! I will not surrender. I will not die curled up in a ball with my hands tied behind my back!" he swore, moaned and then sat on the floor next to me.

Soon Capt. Wanat lost radio contact with the FAC stationed over the battlefield. He tried switching to other antenna.

"I think every antenna is out of service." He turned to Maj. Davidson.

"What are we going to do now? We need to let people outside know we are still alive in here," Maj. Davidson said.

"Should we go outside the bunker to call the FAC?" I suggested. I was not even sure it would work.

"Yeah, let's do it," said Maj. Davidson reluctantly. "We don't have any other choice."

I put my helmet on and grabbed my M16 rifle. I led the way up to the west stairway entrance. The air was permeated with dark smoke and sickening smells. As I stood guard at the inside corner of the six-foot-tall sandbag wall, Capt. Wanat was trying to adjust the radio antenna. Suddenly, I heard something bounce off the sandbag wall and roll down next to my right foot. I looked down. It was a live grenade! Instinctively, I kicked it outside, and it exploded on the other side of the wall.

Soon I heard the rumbling of footsteps approaching. "Quick, they are pushing in!" I screamed as I fired my rifle. The enemy must have seen our movement at the entrance and were about to attack. I kept firing my rifle to prevent them from coming. Then an RPG B40 rocket round exploded on the other side of the sandbag wall, knocking me to the ground. The shrapnel pierced through the stock of Maj. Davidson's M16 rifle and slightly wounded his elbow. I popped in my last magazine and kept firing until it ran out of bullets.

"Let's go!" Capt. Wanat yelled. He had finished the call with the FAC to drop bombs on top of the command bunker. Immediately we retreated to the command bunker to find that it was almost emptied out. Everyone was exiting through the east side stairway.

"Follow them!" I called to Capt. Wanat as he was leading the way.

We raced across the empty room as the NVA rushed in from behind. I heard gunfire behind me as I reached the top of the east stairway. I slammed the heavy wooden door behind me, when several explosions shook the door. The enemy had thrown satchel charges to blow up the empty bunker.

We came to the narrow, open field outside the TOC. The lead group of more than 10 people headed to the front gate. They were immediately mowed down by enemy machine guns positioned inside the compound. Mr. Tuong was among the dead. Seeing what happened with the group in front of us, we turned right and headed toward a hole in the concertina wire fences. I trampled on several NVA dead bodies to reach the other side. As I came to the edge of the airstrip, I looked up and saw a low flying aircraft release a CBU bomb from its wing. It was like slow motion in a movie scene, frame by frame. The bomb exploded in midair, releasing hundreds of bomblets (submunitions) that detonated over a large area of the airstrip. I immediately dove to the ground as they exploded around me. The whole place erupted into a red storm of dirt, shrapnel and smoke. Before the dust subsided, I saw Maj. Davidson get up and turn around as he yelled "Go tell Wanat to stop the bomb run!"

"Yes sir!" I got on my feet and raced across the airstrip. By the time I reached the tree line on the other side, more CBU bomblets exploded behind me. I quickly jumped into a foxhole which Capt. Wanat had occupied. I turned around and saw Maj. Davidson emerging from the big cloud of red dust and smoke, holding two crying babies, one in each hand. His broken rifle kept slipping from his left shoulder and banging on one of the baby's heads.

"Thieu Ta, I'm over here!" I called out to him.

"Where is the mother?" he asked.

"What mother?" I had no idea what he was talking about. I looked around and there was a lady, crying and trembling, coming out from a bush behind me.

"You hold on to these and get the hell out of my way!" Maj. Davidson yelled at her. Then he handed the babies over to her.

Apparently, when the mother saw the bomblets exploding around her, she let go of her babies on the airstrip, then fled for her own life. Maj. Davidson saw the poor, crying babies lying on the ground. He turned around and grabbed one in each of his hands, swinging them by their biceps, and darted across the airstrip as more bombs rained down around them.

We looked at each other in disbelief. There were no wounds on our bodies, not even a trace of blood on our dusty uniforms. Looking back, I can now say how amazed I was that a split second or a single step meant the difference between life and death, but at the time we simply felt fortunate we were not blown to pieces by our friendly airstrike. It truly was a miracle. Even though we were happy to be out of the besieged compound, what happened next would determine whether we would survive the ordeal.

There were 16 of us crowded into four foxholes at the northwest edge of the plantation near the airstrip. The foxholes formed a half circle facing south. The NVA dug them on the first day when they prepared to launch the attack. It was ironic that, as the NVA now took over our totally collapsed compound, we were using their foxholes to get ready for our escape.

I saw a small band of NVA soldiers approaching, about five of them, sneaking around at the tree line from the south. We opened fire at them. I saw one enemy drop to the ground and the rest disappear into the woods. We called for air strikes around our position to keep the enemy at bay. A minute later, a low flying aircraft released a cluster bomb in the direction where the enemy retreated.

It was calm for a while, occasional air strikes still pounding the 9th Regimental Compound. We had lost contact with Capt. "Zippo" Mark Smith and his team. Their situation seemed to be worse than what we had been going through. The whole infantry regiment, apparently, had disintegrated.

As I looked from the foxhole where the three of us were cramped together, I was struck by the magnitude of devastation and destruction a few days of fighting had brought to this small piece of landscape. The French villa had been destroyed, and all but three corners of the two story building still stood, smoke smoldering from the ruin. The district and the 9th ARVN Regiment compounds were still burning. Smoke billowed from every corner of the compounds. There were hundreds of dead bodies and body parts mingled together, friend and foe alike. Some were stacked three high. Among them were children and women. They were scattered inside the barbed wires, on top of the crumbled bunkers, in the openings of bunkers and on the airstrip. They stretched as far as my eyes could see from one end of the airstrip to the other.

Soon I noticed something crawling on the red dirt airstrip and moving slowly toward me. As I looked closely, it was a wounded 9th Regiment ARVN soldier. Both his legs were severed up to his thighs. The wounds were covered with blood and red dirt. His green uniform was torn and stained. He used his arms to lift and slowly push himself, inching forward in agony.

"Brother," he uttered a few words with dry lips that I barely could hear as he came closer to the foxhole where I stayed, "Give me some water to drink."

I was stunned by his humble request. He did not ask for medical help, or anything to ease his pain, all he wanted was a sip of water to quench his thirst!

"Does anyone have water?" I turned around and asked. But none of us had carried a canteen when we rushed out of the compound.

"Sorry, we have no water for you." I turned to him. He seemed disappointed. Then he closed his eyes. He murmured with his dry lips, something that I could hardly hear. He lowered his head until his face dropped to the ground. His body shivered and jerked. Then he lay motionless next to my foxhole.

I had never felt so helpless and guilty in all of my life as I stared at his motionless body. I could not even offer a simple, basic need to a dying stranger. I knew I must treat others with dignity and my faith in God compelled me to defend the helpless and offer help to the neediest. These are the right things to do, no matter what circumstances.

The cruelty of war was not from the bombs or bullets, but in its ability to strip the dignity and humanity from every being — alive or dead, friend or foe — until nothing remained.

– CHAPTER 9 –

Daring Rescue Mission

More than a half an hour went by as we waited in the foxholes. Maj. Davidson was on the radio talking with Maj. Gen. Hollingsworth who was in his command chopper, hovering over the battle field. He was excited to know we escaped the compound alive, and assured us a rescue mission was underway to pick us up from the horrific scene.

"Tinh," Maj. Davidson turned to me. "Tell Maj. Thinh that the U.S. Command is going to pull a rescue mission to pick us up. If the chopper comes, it will only pick up three of us and the district chief. The rest will have to stay."

"Yes sir." I replied and relayed the message to the district chief.

I was overjoyed. It gave me my first glimpse of hope for a long time. Soon I realized any attempt to land a helicopter in any open field near the airstrip would be dangerous, if not suicidal, given the hundreds of enemy anti-aircraft guns positioned on the battlefield. And, even if the chopper landed safely, the rest of Maj. Thinh's men would cling to the overloaded chopper, causing it to be unable to lift off. Nevertheless, I tried not to think about it and hoped for the best outcome.

I leaned against the dirt wall of the foxhole, closely monitoring the radio conversation between Maj. Davidson and Maj. Gen. Hollingsworth.

"This is Danger 79er (Maj. Gen. Hollingsworth). Oh baby, I'm coming pretty good. I'm still fighting and checking. I've been promised it [the rescue chopper] in ten minutes. Don't go anywhere, I know where you are."

"Danger 79er, this is Eighty-three (Maj. Davidson). We're surrounded by Charlies (NVA), get it to us ASAP. Over." He was not convinced.

"Just going as fast as I can. Can you hold out just eight more minutes? I'm working as fast as I can, Eighty-three. Keep down, keep yourself together. You are great. Talked to the FAC (Forward Air Controller) and just hold with it, baby."

"This is Eighty-three. If we got the hell out of here, it would be pure luck. "

"Ah," The general replied. "Bull, don't you worry about that, baby. Well, it is not pure luck, baby. Hang in there. Over."

"Roger." Maj. Davidson replied.

Minutes later, Maj. Gen. Hollingsworth was on the radio again. "Everything is airborne, everything is up now. It is just a matter of a few minutes.... Ah, damn, you are a little strong, great guy, Eighty-three. Just stand by now and listen and keep the net [radio] of yours open and talk to the FACs."[1]

We all held our breath, staring at the sky. Any moment now we would be out of this misery.

Soon I heard the sound of a low flying helicopter careening from the east, followed by the deafening sound of AA guns fire. It cracked across the hot air and thousands of red bullet tracers dotted the cloudy sky from every corner. For a moment, we could not figure out what had happened to the approaching helicopter. Then Maj. Gen. Hollingsworth's voice cracked on the radio again:

"Damn it, he got shot up with 50-cal. (machine gun) fire. We're putting more ordinances on the g--damned things to try to get in there for you."

"We don't have much time." Maj. Davidson replied impatiently.

"Well, I'm going to try it again, hang in there." Maj. Gen. Hollingsworth assured us. He hadn't given up yet.[1]

I saw a low flying, fixed-wing aircraft release a blanket of non-lethal gas. A smoke screen appeared to the east and south near our position. They tried to create a smoke screen for the helicopter to swoop in, but the smoke dissipated in less than a few minutes.

By now it was almost six o'clock in the evening. I heard rumbling engine sounds coming from the south end of the airstrip. I leaned my head outside of the foxhole. I saw four Russian-made T54 tanks lumbering toward us, their turrets pointed in our direction. Obviously, they were coming after us.

"Look, tanks are coming!" I screamed.

"Are you sure?" someone asked.

"Yes, they are." One of Maj. Thinh's body guards got out of his foxhole and confirmed what I saw. "Oh, no, we'd better get the hell out of here!"

We all, simultaneously, got out of the foxholes.

Maj. Davidson radioed Maj. Gen. Hollingsworth and told him what was happening and that we could not wait any longer.

"Eighty-three [you] stick with the little people, and keep that radio on. Out." Maj. Gen. Hollingsworth replied.[1]

It was the last radio communication we would have with the outside world.

CHAPTER 10

Escape from the Inferno

We headed east along the tree line. At about six o'clock we reached a small, abandoned brick ranch house not far from QL-13. The house was still intact. We broke down the front door to find it almost empty except for an ice box in the kitchen that contained a few welcome bottles of soda pop. Someone found some used clothing and gave me an orange flowered T-shirt. I put it on inside of my uniform.

By nightfall, Maj. Davidson, Capt. Wanat, Maj. Thinh and I huddled together behind the house to plan an escape route. The quickest route was to follow QL-13 heading south. This would take us to An Loc within two days. But by now there was no doubt the NVA had totally swamped the whole region. We had to proceed with caution. Our radio's battery was out, so we decided to destroy it before it fell into enemy hands. We dismantled our rifles since none of us had any bullets left. Then we assigned passwords to everyone in the group: challenge with *doc lap* (independence) and reply with *tu do* (freedom).

Under cover of darkness, we moved out of the house in a single column. A pack of Maj. Thinh's men led the front, followed by Maj. Thinh and his S3 officer, Capt. Tam. Capt. Wanat was in front of me and behind me were Maj. Davidson, an RF lieutenant whom I had never met before, and two other soldiers assigned to protect the rear.

It was pitch dark as we marched quietly along QL-13 heading south.

I soon realized it was one of the dumbest decisions we had made. As we slowly crept along the red dirt road under the moonless sky, I soon lost sight of the man in front of me. I stopped on the side of the road and looked around. I saw a dark figure standing 20 yards away on the front porch of a house to my left, I challenged him with my password, and he replied *doan khet* (unity).

I turned around and screamed, "Run!" Bullets zipped over my head as we ran back to where we came from. Apparently we had run into an NVA guard post. I stood on the road and looked around again. There was no one else except me, Maj. Davidson and the three Vietnamese soldiers who were behind us at the end of the column. We were completely cut off from Capt. Wanat and the other men in the front. The RF lieutenant and two other soldiers were all shaken up and started walking away from us. I asked them where they were going.

"We're going to the town square. I'm not staying with you guys. It's too dangerous," the lieutenant said. Without looking back, they disappeared into the dark. Maj. Davidson and myself were left standing in the middle of the road.

"Tinh," said Maj. Davidson, holding my left arm and pulling me. "Don't leave me alone here!" He, too, was shaken up.

"Sir, I will not," I turned and assured him "Thieu Ta, we both came together and now we will flee together. However," I continued, "two things we must remember. First, we must trust in God, and secondly, be patient. It may take a couple of days or even a week to get to An Loc. Who knows what we'll run into next."

Maj. Davidson nodded.

Suddenly a group of armed NVA emerged from a dark alley on the west side of the road and started running toward us. We both quickly jumped into a nearby ditch. They ran past us and headed south where we were ambushed a few minutes earlier. A loud explosion lit up the area and gunfire rang out in the calm of the night.

"They probably got Wanat and Maj. Thinh," Maj. Davidson said.

"Yeah, it looks like they are in trouble," I replied. "We had better stay away from the road — as far away as possible."

Timing was critical. There was no doubt in our minds that the enemy's next target would be An Loc. If we took too long to get out of what was now enemy territory, we would find a war zone instead of rescue in An Loc.

We climbed out of the ditch, headed east, passed through an alley between two houses and into a backyard garden full of banana trees. I looked up and saw an AC-130 Spectre gunship hovering high overhead, well beyond the range of anti-aircraft guns. Its bright, powerful searchlight beamed back and forth in the dark sky looking for suspicious targets on the ground. Suddenly it moved toward where we were standing. We ran for cover under the shade of a banana tree, lying flat on the ground and pretending to be dead. I closed my eyes, held my breath and hoped for the best. Any movement on our part would make us a deadly target.

The search light circled over us for a moment, and then moved away. We took advantage of that split second of darkness, got up, and jumped into a creek a few yards away as we watched the searchlight return to the same spot where we were before. The thought of being shot by this giant flying monster, particularly by its merciless XM134 Vulcan mini-guns, was horrifying. It could fire up to 4,000 rounds per minute. I had seen the victims of this deadly weapon. It was quite messy, to say the least.

Soon the mini-gun exploded from the aircraft, and hit a target less than two hundred yards away, with the Spectres' 105mm cannon joining in to pound the target below. The enemy responded with AA guns and small arms fire, to no effect. The exchange of fire turned the dark sky into a "Fourth of July" firecracker display. Then a huge orange and red fireball seared upward, one of the rounds apparently hitting an explosive target on the ground.

We took advantage of the skirmish to get out of the creek and walk away from the hot spot. We climbed to the top of a small hill, too exhausted to move on. We lay flat near an open field under the dark sky, and tried to sleep. Overnight, I heard the rumbling sound of bomb explosions to the south.

Early on the dawn of April 8 we decided to find a place to hide for the day and move out again when evening came. Near the slope of the hill was a bamboo bush. It was green and dense; an ideal place for hiding. Besides, from there we could see several seemingly abandoned houses in the valley below which, presumably, could be an ideal place to find food and water. We settled in for a little while.

As we were getting ready to descend to the valley, I saw two military trucks screech to a halt in front of the houses down in the valley. Several NVA soldiers got off and started unloading stuff, as if they were moving into the houses. We abandoned the plan and tried to figure out another way to deal with our hunger and thirst. Maj. Davidson took out his pocket knife, the only sharp object we had, to scale a hole in the bamboo branch in hope to find some juice, but it was as dry as desert sand. As the day went by, the air was steamy hot. Thirst and hunger took a toll on our strength. The only comfort we had was the shade of the bamboo bush shielding us from the hot, blazing sun. Now we had to sit idly in the shade of the bush, unable to move around.

At noon Maj. Davidson stood up to stretch his legs. Suddenly, he came down and turned to me. "Shh! VC," he pointed behind me.

"How many of them?" I asked, breathlessly.

"One, standing guard." He replied.

"How far?" I asked again.

"One hundred yards."

There was not much we could do except wait for darkness in order to get away from this madness.

At nightfall we crawled out from the bamboo bush. We headed north, away from the NVA guard station behind the bamboo bush, and turned east into the woods. Our most critical need at the moment was drinking water. We stumbled around in the woods for more than an hour, kicking around in the dried beds of the irrigation ditches. There was nothing except leaves and debris. We had not had a sip of water for more than 24 hours. Our thirst took precedence over everything else. We stood in the middle of an opening in the woods, too tired to walk another step. I stared at the starless sky and hallucinated that it had suddenly opened up and poured rain.

"God! I need water!" I panted. My mouth was so dry that I felt as if it was on fire. I dropped to the ground and lay there, not knowing how much time had gone by. Suddenly, I felt a cool breeze and the wind started to pick up. I looked up. The sky was swirling with thick, dark clouds. Lighting flashed and zipped across the sky accompanied by deafening thunder. First there was only a few drops, and then the rain poured as if the sky was opening the flood gate. I slowly got up and walked around with my mouth wide open and sucked in the cool and refreshing water. I stretched my hands out, dancing and rejoicing in God's timely providence. Maj. Davidson was standing still, lifting his head high. Our uniforms were soaked and the downpour washed off the filth, smell and horrors of the past few days.

"Strange," I murmured to myself, "the monsoon season in this part of the country would not begin for another month. How could it come so soon?"

For the next four days of our escape, the heavy rain not only provided for our thirst, it also covered our movement as we made our way through the enemy territory.

We were so caught up with the downpour we forgot about where we were and in what direction we had to travel. From what I could remember, we were somewhere near Ninh Thanh Hamlet, two miles east of downtown Loc Ninh. We assumed by the sound of explosions and flashes of light on the horizon that we must be south. The fighting, by now, had moved to An Loc.

– CHAPTER 11 –

In the Presence of My Enemy

We followed a small trail leading into a rubber plantation some-where nearby. It seemed much darker in the woods with the rain pouring down hard. I could hardly see anything in front of me. We stumbled among rubber trees and, at times, fell into the irrigation ditches in between the rows of trees. Suddenly, there were faint points of light from many flashlights pointing at us from all directions. I tried to convince myself that it was a friendly unit still hanging around in the woods. Given what happened during the past few days, this was impossible because all friendly units in the area had either disinte-grated or surrendered.

"Oh, no! It is over." I thought to myself.

"Tinh, We are surrounded!" I felt Maj. Davidson squeeze my arm. His voice trembled.

I was so scared and my whole body was shaking. My brain froze, my legs seemed to melt like wax and my knees knocked together. Obvi-ously, we had stumbled into the middle of a large enemy defensive position. We both took few steps back, and I felt my feet fall out from underneath me. We tumbled into a ditch.

As we got up and tried to get away from the confrontation, I heard a gentle voice calling me. *"Tinh, come this way!"* It was so clear, as if someone had whispered into my ear. I turned around and followed the voice. Maj. Davidson walked next to me. Suddenly I realized that, since the beginning of the fighting, we were *not* alone. There was another person — God, or His angel — with us. Sometimes we think of the Creator as transcendent, always too far beyond our reach. In fact, He desires to be close to us, ever present in our lives. God is always at my side leading the way, even in the darkest moments of my life.

The next half an hour seemed to last an eternity as the dim flashlights still pointed at us from all directions. The three of us kept moving forward in the pitch black woods under heavy rain. My fear had completely disappeared. In its place was a feeling of peace that overwhelmed me. I was living through Psalm 23: *"Even when I walk through the dark valley of death, I will not be afraid, for you are close beside me.... You prepare a feast for me in the presence of my enemies."*

At that moment I realized that God, who had once shut the mouths of lions for Daniel, would also, on this night, blind the eyes of my enemy. I promised myself I would change my name to Daniel if I ever got out of this place alive.

Under cover of the heavy rain, we passed through the enemy camp. Soon I heard the sound of rushing water to my right. To my surprise, there was a small creek near the edge of the rubber plantation. The water was only knee deep. We decided to creep into the creek in order to avoid running into the enemy again. We trod quite a distance until I heard a rustling sound behind the bushes at my right on the bank of the creek. With each flash of lightning, I identified three figures dressed in uniforms. Two of them were holding AK47 rifles, and the other had a B-40 grenade launcher. They were trailing us. As we moved forward, they followed. Whenever we stopped, they, too, stopped. But for some reason, they did not open fire. Why would they think a pair of men treading through a creek on this dark, rainy night was not worth challenging?

I signaled to Maj. Davidson that we must submerge under the water in order to break away from them. After a while I looked around again to find we were alone. Physically and emotionally drained, we climbed out of the creek, and fell asleep on the ground.

When daylight came on April 9, the rain stopped. We found ourselves in the garden of a farm. There was a straw shack in the middle of the property surrounded with fruit trees and flower beds. The shack had no door or window except for a small opening in the front and another in the rear. Outside of the shack was a primitive, below-ground bomb shelter. It was about 20 feet by 15 feet, three feet deep, covered with a bamboo plank, with an old straw mat coiled up inside. There was a breadfruit tree nearby with a few thorny, green and yellow fruits hanging low. I walked over and picked two from the tree. At least I had something to fill my stomach.

We walked toward the shack and I looked inside. A wooden plank bed was set up by the back wall. It was covered with a mosquito net and a blanket was spread over it. There was a pair of rubber sandals under the bed. The room was dark and I did not see anyone inside. A teapot sat idle on the wood stove in the small kitchen at the right corner of the room. We assumed the shack was abandoned, so we decided to hide in the primitive bomb shelter next to it.

We crouched low and tried to cover ourselves with the old straw mat, but Maj. Davidson had a hard time to keeping his head down.

Suddenly I heard the voice again. *"Get out!"*

Simultaneously, we crawled out of the shelter and started walking toward the shack. At that very moment, I saw seven to ten NVA soldiers walking through the front gate toward us. We quickly turned around and ran toward a fence in the backyard. Near the fence was a ditch filled with water from the rain the night before. We jumped into the muddy ditch and tried to get away from the farm. Near the ditch was a tree lying on the ground. Its leaves were freshly green and dense and the trunk rested on top of a stump. We panicked, much like a mouse who could not find its mouse hole. Without even thinking, we crawled under the downed tree and lay flat on our backs. Maj. Davidson was on my left side. We spread the loose leaves to cover our bodies as much as possible. I took off my eyeglasses so that no reflection could give away our hiding place. The tree was barely large enough to cover both of us from head to toe, we had to be so tight that there was no room to turn around. It was not the best place to hide, but under this circumstance I could not ask for anything better.

We hid side by side. All day long we just stared through the branches at the blue, cloudy sky above. The weather was not hot, but it was humid after the torrential rains. I noticed two small, dark finches hopping from one branch to another over my head. They were poking around for something from the tree branches, then flew away and returned for more.

I never thought that I could have such a relaxing moment in enemy territory, lying on my back, watching these two little creatures for entertainment. They frisked around, doing their routine. At times, they turned their heads and stared at us with their little black eyes as if wondering why two men were lying so still under their tree. They were free to soar to the treetops and dance and sing to their hearts' content. They enjoyed their surroundings without any thoughts of hostility. How unlike their human counterparts who hid nervously under the tree, hungry and desperate to avoid being captured by their enemy.

I was awakened by the rumbling of footsteps. I overheard someone bark out his order to search the farm. They had discovered our combat boot prints in the courtyard. We held our breath as they moved around near the tree where we were hiding. Then I heard someone chopping wood in the backyard. What if they came to the tree where we hid? I thought to myself, "Wouldn't they be surprised to find two strangers lying nervously underneath?"

By noon, they stopped the wood chopping and went for lunch.

All day long I wondered why the NVA troops kept walking back and forth on my right. At one time, more than 30 of them marched by. They came so close that I could clearly recognize the scars on some of their faces, even though I had removed my eyeglasses. I could easily trip one of them if I stretched out my right hand. Soon I realized our tree was next to a small trail that connected to the neighboring farm. There was not much I could do but keep quiet and stay still.

We lay there motionless. At one point, Maj. Davidson elbowed me. I turned my head and saw an ugly, black centipede crawling across his forehead. He held his head still until that hairy thing passed, without making any noise.

Time seemed to drag on forever. I thought of my family, especially my mom and dad. How would they feel when they received the news that I was missing in action? I turned my head and looked at Maj. Davidson. I saw tears running down his cheeks. His hand gripped tightly around a cross on his chest.

"I'm thinking of my wife and kids," he whispered when he noticed I was staring at him.

"I'm thinking of my family too," I murmured.

It started to rain again at about six o'clock that evening and soon it was dark. Under the cover of darkness and rain, we crawled out from under the tree. We found the way back to the creek where we were the night before, and slipped into the waist-deep water. We started wading away from the farm.

Soon, Maj. Davidson murmured into my ear. "Tinh, someone is behind me." His voice was tense.

"No, Thieu Ta, there is nobody except you and me." I walked around to assure him.

"Yes, his hand is on my shoulder. I'm going to kill that S.O.B.!" He took out his pocket knife and raised his right hand to grab whatever was on his left shoulder. To his surprise he found a black centipede in his hand. We could not help but laugh at each other.

We moved for about two hours in the creek then climbed back onto dry ground again. As I leaned against a tree stump, I felt a lot of little bugs crawling all over my body. To my surprise, I was sitting on an anthill. I jumped back into the creek to wash them off.

By daybreak on April 10, I recognized we were in the Tom Buor Creek. It ran north and south, parallel with QL-13. It would be an excellent landmark to follow when we needed to move south again when night fell. We found a dense bush on the slope near the creek, away from any trail or houses. It was an ideal place to hide until dark. There was nothing else we could do but sleep, chat and wait for dusk.

By four o'clock in the afternoon, I heard a fixed-wing aircraft fly-ing overhead, followed by a low-flying jet. Then several high, scream-ing whistles followed by explosions that shocked us off the ground. Debris and tree branches rained down on us, so intense that I thought we were going to be buried alive. Then I heard people screaming and yelling not far from behind. AA guns started blasting the air. More bombs exploded. Each bomb fell closer and closer to our hiding place. I turned around and used my hands to lift myself up to absorb the shock waves. I held my breath as I waited for the next wave of bombs that were sure to fall on my head. I closed my eyes and braced for the worst. When, suddenly, everything turned silent.

I still heard the engine sound of the fixed-wing aircraft high in the sky, but the bombers had left the area. I heard the noises of NVA sol-diers not far from where we hid. They were running around, carrying the wounded or dead away, and re-supplying the AA position with more ammunition. By late afternoon the rain came again, bringing needed water and washing our dust-filled clothes.

Night came and we headed out to Tom Buor Creek again. Initially the water was only knee high and I had no problem wading through it. However, there was an awful, foul smell permeating the air. Soon I saw an object float by. In the dark, I touched it and discovered it was a dead body. Then several more floated by. I could not recognize who they were, but the smell was so terribly awful it made me vomit and shiver.

Soon the water became deep and covered my head, I tried to swim, but I was swept away by the rapid current. Maj. Davidson saw me just about to go under. He wrapped his arms around me and pulled me out from the creek. In rescuing me, he broke one of his ribs.

We found a trail running parallel with the creek. We decided to follow the trail. It wound through the backyards of some of the houses, but the rain still poured so heavily that it was unlikely anyone would notice our movement in the dark.

By the next morning, April 11, I found myself sitting in the middle of an open field on higher ground. I stood up and looked around. From this vantage point I saw QL-13, like a brown snake, winding between green tree lines. Further north was Thien Phat hamlet, the small roadside village we had passed on our way to Loc Ninh a week earlier.

"Thieu Ta, over there is Thien Phat hamlet." I pointed to a cluster of houses with their shiny, new tin roofs reflecting the morning sun.

Maj. Davidson got up and looked over in the same direction.

"How far did we go?"

"Not that far — maybe about three kilometers. I think we have been wandering around in the woods in the dark for the last three days, making very little progress. At this pace, it might take another week to get to An Loc."

"Well, it is not a good idea," Maj. Davidson shook his head, "but we might have to start walking in daylight."

"Yeah." I felt uneasy, but agreed with him "You know it means a lot more risk."

"It is still better than wandering in the dark, not knowing where we are going. Besides, An Loc will have fallen if we keep traveling at this rate. If that happens, we will have to go further south to Chon Thanh."

We headed down a winding trail leading south. Soon we came near a black pepper farm. A lady dressed in a white blouse, wearing a cone shaped hat, was riding a bicycle toward us. We both jumped into a bush for cover next to the trail and waited for her to go by. Near the fence of the farm were several tall papaya trees. I looked up and saw a few ripe papayas dangling high on one of the trees. We both shook the tree until one papaya felt to the ground and it split in half. I took a piece — it was so juicy and sweet like honey. I loved every bite of it.

"Horrible!" Maj. Davidson spit it on the ground and threw the rest away after one bite.

It was the first time I had eaten anything in the past five days.

We continued following the trail through a heavy wooded area. Then we came to a large open rice field. I stood at the edge and looked around. Not far from where I stood was an old man dressed in black, sitting in a straw stall by the edge of the woods. Apparently he was by himself, unpacking his lunch. I told Maj. Davidson I wanted to talk to the old man, and I needed his pocket knife.

"If he acts stupidly or screams, I will cut his throat," I swore.

"Be careful!" He handed me the only weapon we had.

I approached him from behind. The old man turned around and saw me and an American approaching him. He was surprised yet calm.

"*Chao cu* (Hello, sir)," I greeted him politely.

"*Chao thay* (Hi, gentleman)," he bowed his head and reached out both of his hands.

"You want to have some rice?" he hesitated a moment, then offered me his only bowl of rice, mixed with vegetables.

"No, thank you," I said, realizing the food he had was barely enough for him.

"Where are you from?" I asked.

"Long Be Hamlet. It is not that far from here." He pointed to the other side of the rice field. Long Be was a small montagnard hamlet. More than a year prior, the local government relocated the hamlet to the present site from a contested area further east. Now a PF squad provided security to the residents.

"I was there last year with the province chief to distribute rice and cooking oil to the refugees." I said.

"Really, I was there too, but I do not remember seeing you." He answered with a smile. Now he felt more willing to talk when I told him I was from the provincial capital.

"Have you seen any VC in this area lately?" I changed the subject.

"Yes, there are many of them. Four days ago the North Vietnamese came into Long Be and started killing the hamlet chief and soldiers stationed there. Some escaped along with their families. The entire village fled to An Loc, except a few old folks like me, who stayed behind."

"Have you heard anything from the group that left for An Loc?"

"No." he answered "I do not know whether they made it there or not."

"Do you know which way they fled to An Loc?"

"They said they would follow the railroad tracks over there." He pointed to the wood on the other side of the rice field.

I turned to Maj. Davidson and explained what the old man had just told me. I remembered there was an abandoned railroad track, located on the east side, running parallel with QL-13, between An Loc and Loc Ninh. By now it would have been covered with heavy vegetation and would not be easy to find.

I looked around at the newly harvested rice paddy. The distance from where we stood to the woods on the other side was about a half-mile-long stretch of wide open field. There was not a single tree or shade for cover in between. Crossing the field in broad daylight was not impossible, but would take some risk of exposing ourselves to the enemy nearby.

"I think we just go for it." Maj. Davidson said.

I thanked the old man for his help and asked him to stay there until we reached the other side of the field.

"Don't worry about me, you just go. May *Ong Troi* (the Heaven) protect you," he assured me and waved with a smile.

We followed the muddy, uneven rice paddy dikes and dashed across the open field. As we reached the tree line on the other side, we were gasping for air and exhausted. After a while we looked around to make sure no one had followed us before we moved into the dense wood.

We plowed through heavy jungle for almost two hours, exhausted and thirsty. My blistered feet started to hurt. The air was hot, even under the shade of a canopy of vegetation. Thirst took a toll on me. I began to see a stream of rushing water flowing right before my eyes. I tried to reach for it, but there was nothing there. Soon I dropped to the ground, too exhausted to drag my feet another step.

"Come on Tinh, see what happens when you eat too much rice?" Maj. Davidson teased me. He was tired, yet his physical endurance and strength made him in much better shape than me.

We came upon an old bomb crater that was half filled with filthy water. The water had already turned into a rusty, blue colored pond, and there were insects floating on top of it. We both looked at each other, then stared at the filthy pond. There was not much choice. We needed a sip of water so badly, something to wet our burning mouths. We knelt down, lapped the water with our hands and sipped with our tongues, to moisten our dry lips.

About an hour later we reached Can Lo Creek. The water was cool and clean. We drank as much as we could, then rested on the bank before moving out again. Can Lo was just five miles from An Loc. If things went well, we could reach the city before dark.

We continued heading south and soon we found the abandoned

railroad tracks. The track had not been used since the beginning of the war. The rails were quite rusty, but the wooden ties were still intact. Overgrown vegetation created a dense canopy, completely covering the tracks that were now not easily seen from the air. Food packages, helmets, backpacks, and even a few rotted bodies were scattered along the rusty tracks, an indication of a brutal ambush that had taken place in the vicinity few days earlier.

We followed the railroad tracks for a little while when I sensed something was not right. "Thieu Ta, I have a gut feeling that we should stay away from the tracks."

"Yeah, good idea, or we might run into an ambush just like those dead guys."

We got off the railroad tracks, and headed into the dense woods again. By five o'clock in the afternoon, we reached the rubber plantation outside of An Loc near QL-13.

I stood near the edge of the plantation, and from there I could see the city of An Loc sitting on a hill. There was no sound of gunfire or explosions. A few pillars of smoke rose from the center of the town. Had the city already been overrun by the NVA or was it still in South Vietnamese hands? It was hard to tell from this distance. The only way to find out was to go there.

I decided to take off my uniform. The stench was unbearable, and it had started irritating my sensitive skin. I sat on the ground and took off my boots to check my feet. They were pale white and wrinkled with a few blisters on the sides, and both heels were turning red and swollen. It was not as bad as I had thought. Maj. Davidson insisted that he would not take off his uniform. He said he was so proud to wear it, regardless of whether he was dead or alive.

"How about if we take this road to An Loc?" Maj. Davidson asked me as he walked toward the now, apparently, deserted QL-13.

"Why not, we could reach the city before dark," I answered as I put my boots back on.

It was quiet, except for the sound of our heavy steps trodding on the uneven pavement. Many landmines were shallowly buried on the road. Their detonators were poking out from the surface after the recent torrential rain had washed off the layer of red dirt that covered them. As I tried to avoid stepping on the mines, I heard squeaking noises behind me. I turned around and saw an old man, dressed in black, who looked like a typical farmer. He was wearing a conical hat and riding a rusty bicycle. He navigated around the deadly landmines with surprising ease to climb the uphill road.

What was this old man doing? I wondered. Why was he riding a bike on this abandoned road filled with landmines in the middle of the battlefield? I can say of all the things I had seen in the war in recent years, the sight of this old man was the most ridiculous.

He saw me standing there staring at him. "Hey, *cau* (young man), I give you a ride to the city. It is getting late." He glanced at me and gasped for air as he stopped in front of me.

"I appreciate that, but I'm with him." I tried to be polite as I pointed to Maj. Davidson.

He looked at Maj. Davidson then picked up speed and disappeared into the fading dusk.

It was already past six o'clock and pitch dark. We were another mile away from the city limits. Suddenly, someone shouted out very loudly in Vietnamese from a distance. "Stop! Do not move or I will open fire!"

I froze in the middle of the road not knowing what to do. Maj. Davidson kept pulling my arm trying to get me into a ditch on the side of the road.

"Tinh, let's run for cover," he was frightened and panicky. "I'll never allow them to get me after I have gone this far to avoid being captured. No way! No way!"

"No, Thieu Ta, don't do it, they are going to open fire and kill us if we run. Look, there is no place to hide!" I tried to calm him down as I pointed to the open field on both sides of the road.

Maj. Davidson jumped into the ditch, then climbed back out again and tried to pull me off the road.

"Do not run or we will open fire!" they shouted again in the dark.

"Thieu Ta, give me a chance me talk to them." I tried to talk, but he kept interrupting me.

I sensed something familiar in the menacing voice. They spoke in the southern dialect, and their tone was somewhat friendly.

"*Anh oi,* (Hey, brother)," I yelled out in Vietnamese. "I am standing here with no weapon or anything, and I don't know where you are. Would you send someone here to talk to me?"

"Are you with an American?" they asked.

How could they know I was with an American? I wondered. Could it be that the old man on the bike who we passed by earlier told them we were coming up the road behind him? Nevertheless, their southern dialect and friendly tone gave me some hints that they might be a friendly unit defending the city.

Meanwhile, Maj. Davidson kept on pulling me and insisting that I must run with him.

"Thieu Ta, you must let me talk to them." I resisted. I lost my patience.

"Would you send someone here to talk to me now?" I called out again.

"OK, we are coming. Don't do anything stupid or I will open fire."

In the faint darkness I heard heavy treading sounds, and then I saw four figures moving closer with their rifles pointed at us. At first I recognized the outline of their steel helmets, typical ARVN soldier military gear (the VC or NVA only wore green jungle pith helmets). As they came closer, I saw their uniforms had a black panther head insignia on their sleeves. They introduced themselves as a ranger unit from the ARVN 3rd Ranger Group.

I was excited to see the faces of friendly forces for the first time in the past four days. They ordered us to follow them to their command post immediately. They said it was not safe to stand on the road.

I turned around. I found Maj. Davidson in the ditch again.

"Thieu Ta, they are a friendly Ranger unit!" I tried to convince him with the good news.

He jumped out from the ditch and grasped the shoulder of one of the soldiers and started barking at him.

"How do you know they are friendly? Do they know who the province chief is? Who the *co van* (advisor) is?"

Then from behind came an ARVN officer who could speak some broken English "Hey you! We are Rangers!" he yelled at Maj. Davidson, as he flashed a light on the black panther head shoulder patch on his uniform.

We were saved!

Finally, after Maj. Davidson calmed down, we followed them to a defensive position on high ground near the road. The officer introduced himself as 2nd Lt. Tran Tan Phuoc, a platoon leader of the 31st Ranger Battalion, 3rd Ranger Group. They arrived at An Loc two days earlier to reinforce the besieged city. He also told me he picked up Maj. Thinh, the Loc Ninh District Chief, that morning. When I asked him if there was an American with him, he said the district chief came in by himself.

Lt. Phuoc immediately informed his headquarters of our arrival and requested their advisors to contact the Provincial Advisory Team of our safe return. Soon Lt. Col. Robert Corley was on the radio and assured us someone would pick us up first thing in the morning. I asked Lt. Phuoc for food. He told me they had run out of food that morning. The Province Chief promised them some rations, but it never arrived. Instead, he gave me his water canteen and offered us his shelter to stay for the night. He led us to a small tin-roofed shed up the hill. Inside was a shallow hole in the ground, big enough for Maj. Davidson and myself to sit upright in there. Lt. Phuoc told us to keep our heads down because the NVA constantly shelled his defensive position. His men would secure the perimeter for the night.

Throughout the night the NVA were firing mortars and rockets into our position. The shelling rattled the tin roof of the shed and punched a few more shrapnel holes into the already shabby wall. Nevertheless, Maj. Davidson and I slept through it, and I felt much safer in the hands of ARVN forces.

– CHAPTER 12 –

Going Home

The morning of April 12 was sunny. Maj. Davidson and I walked out of the shed to catch some fresh air. We sat on the ground over-looking QL-13. It was quiet. Apparently both sides were exhausted from the overnight exchange of fire. Over to the left I saw Lt. Phuoc sitting next to a foxhole, puffing a cigarette, while a few of his men slept in a dugout. When he saw both of us sitting there, he came over and sat next to me.

"How was last night?" he asked. His sleepless, weary eyes revealed the fact that he had not slept through the night.

"It was good — in fact, it was the first time I could sleep like a baby for a long time," I answered.

I thanked him for not firing on us when we ran into his men on the road the night before. I also told him we almost slipped away while his men were yelling at us.

"Wow, you guys were lucky you didn't," he looked at me and Maj. Davidson. "There were mines and booby traps all along both sides of the road. You could have been blown to pieces!"

"How could you know I was with an American on the road in the night?" I was curious.

"There was a…" Our conversation was disrupted by the sound of engines rattling the calm morning. I saw two black Honda scooters heading out from the city, zigzagging on the pothole-filled road, a cloud of red dust trailing behind them.

"Look! They're coming to pick you up." Lt. Phuoc said.

We stood up and started walking toward the road. Suddenly, several mortar rounds exploded on the road near the scooters. The riders immediately threw down their scooters and jumped into a ditch nearby. We, also, lay down on the ground. The shelling stopped momentarily so we got up and ran to the road. The riders remounted their scooters and Maj. Davidson and I hopped on behind them. As we sped into the city, more mortar rounds exploded behind us.

I will never forget Lt. Phuoc and his men for their courage and hospitality during the last, crucial moments of our escape, and what happened to his platoon the day after we left An Loc. The next morning, April 13, the NVA had launched a major offensive to capture the city of An Loc. Lt. Phuoc and his men took the first punch of slaughter. Many months later I read a report that his unit was almost wiped out on that fatal morning. Only he and two of his men survived the initial attack. A few months later, Lt. Phuoc was killed in a battle when his unit tried to retake the city. I feel a sense of loss every time I think of Lt. Phuoc and his men. They willingly risked their own lives to bring us back home safely. They protected and sheltered us in the midst of a fierce battle. They have my gratitude and I still owe them a debt I will not be able to repay.

The motorcycles wound through the familiar streets of An Loc, heading south to the provincial headquarters. The streets were filled with soldiers and civilians who stopped what they were doing and stared at us as we sped by. The fear of an imminent attack was clearly written on everyone's face. At every corner, ARVN soldiers were busy filling sandbags to re-enforce their defensive lines, preparing for a protracted battle never before seen during the entire Vietnam War.

We arrived at the fortified provincial military headquarters compound south of the city. I thanked the soldiers for risking their lives to pick us up. Maj. Davidson got off the motorcycle and fell to the ground. He was too tired to walk another step. Col. Tran Van Nhut, the Province Chief, who happened to be walking by, carried Maj. Davidson to his command bunker.

"Corley, I've got your man!" said Col. Nhut he as entered the command bunker and put Maj. Davidson in a chair. The whole place was rejoicing for our safe return. However, they were still waiting for news of the remaining advisors. (Reports later indicated that Capt. George K. Wanat, Maj. Albert E. Carlson, Capt. Mark A. "Zippo" Smith, Sgt. Kenneth Wallingford and the French reporter, Yves Michel Dumond, were captured. Both Lt. Col. Richard Schott and Sgt. 1st Class Howard Lull were killed in action.)

Lt. Col. Corley came over to give me a hug. He told me a helicopter would arrive soon to take us to the hospital for a physical checkup.

Col. Nhut also congratulated me on a job well done and wished me a speedy recovery. Many of my colleagues came over to congratulate me. Someone gave me a bottle of soda.

Maj. Robert Blair accompanied us to the soccer field that was now turned into helicopter landing zone just across the street from the headquarters compound. He returned from R&R vacation to find that his post in Loc Ninh no longer existed. He was reassigned to set up a temporary office for all nonessential advisory team personnel in Bien Hoa until the situation in An Loc returned to normal.

We crouched in a freshly dug foxhole on the red dirt soccer field and waited for the flight. Enemy rockets and artillery rounds were constantly pounding the city and, especially, the soccer field when the helicopter approached for landing. I watched a Huey helicopter, escorted by two Cobra gunships, flying low over the tree tops approaching from the west. Immediately, sound of anti-aircraft guns rattled the bright, morning sky and the gunships returned fire to the wood below. The enemy would shoot at every aircraft flying in or out. Finally, the Huey helicopter touched down on the soccer field long enough to unload its cargo as we climbed aboard. It took off before we could fasten the seat belts. We flew up, hugging the tree tops, and headed south. The M-60 machine guns onboard, joined by the two Cobra gunships, fired into the rubber plantation below to suppress the enemy fire. Maj. Blair handed a note to the pilot to take us directly to Maj. Gen. Hollingsworth's office at the Third Regional Assistance Command (TRAC) headquarters in Long Binh Base.

It is undeniable that our escape was a miracle. God had planned every detail, even down to the timing of our arrival at the besieged city of An Loc the night before. As many reports indicated later, on April 6, the day before the NVA overran our position in Loc Ninh, two elite NVA divisions (the 7th NVA and 9th VC) and their armor, artillery and anti-aircraft support elements, had reached An Loc under cover of darkness and took up positions encircling the provincial capital. They had ample time, manpower and fire support ready and were capable to launch an attack at a moment's notice. Instead, for some unknown reason, or as indicated in some after-action reports, they waited for more supplies. They sat and did nothing for an entire week, wasting a precious opportunity of surprise attack, while the city was still scrambling to bring in reinforcements. The enemy's delay had given Maj. Davidson and I just enough time to reach An Loc safely. Less than 24 hours after the moment our helicopter took off from the soccer field the enemy launched a ground attack. For the next 66 days they turned this once beloved city into hell.

The helicopter landed at the TRAC's VIP pad. Brig. Gen. John R. McGriffert, the Deputy Commanding General of TRAC, greeted us at his office. Maj. Davidson made a phone call to his wife and family in the States.

Brig. Gen. John R. McGriffert (left), greeted us at
Third Regional Assistance Command Headquarters,
Long Binh Base, Bien Hoa, South Vietnam, April 12, 1972

For the next two days Maj. Davidson and I received physical check-ups and recuperated at the base. Maj. Davidson suffered only minor cuts on his elbows and a broken rib. I was in pretty decent shape except for my blistered feet. I only weighed 90 lbs.

On April 14, Maj. Davidson and I stood at a medal presentation ceremony at 3rd ARVN Military Region (MR3) Headquarters in Bien Hoa province. Maj. Gen. Hollingsworth and Brig. Gen. Nguen Van Hieu, the deputy commanding general of MR3, presided over the ceremony in the presence of Vietnamese officers and members of Advisory Team 47. Maj. Davidson was awarded the Distinguished Service Cross Medal, a Purple Heart Medal, and the ARVN Gallantry Cross Medal with cluster leaves. I was presented a Silver Star Medal for combat valor, the third highest decoration in the U.S. army, and the ARVN Gallantry Cross Medal with Gold Star.

After the ceremony, Maj. Davidson informed me he had received orders to return to the States that afternoon. We chatted and joked for a while and reminded each other not to forget what the Lord had done for us. I told him it was a great honor to serve with him and wished him and his family the best.

Medal presentation ceremony at 3rd ARVN Military Region Headquarters, Bien Hoa, South Vietnam, April 14, 1972. (Front, l.-r.): Maj. Gen. Hollingsworth, SFC Tinh (Daniel Luc, the author), and Maj. Davidson.

The next day I reported to the MR3 headquarters and was granted a seven-day leave to recuperate at home. I took a bus to Cho Lon where my parents lived and arrived home about six o'clock in the evening.

My mom opened the door.

She looked at me from my head to my toes, "Tinh, did you lose weight?"

"Mom, I'm fine." I tried to avoid her question. I gave her the medals I had just received and a bag of candy I bought.

I walked to the dining room to find my sister Mai setting the table for dinner.

"Mom prepared this dish for you. She said you would be home today," Mai said as she placed a plate of soy sauce chicken on the table. The familiar aroma of my favorite dish reminded me that I was truly home again.

"How could she know I was coming home today?" I puzzled.

"Well, I don't know, but mom always knows."

I stared at my favorite dish on the table. My mom neither read Chinese nor spoke Vietnamese, although she picked up a Chinese newspaper every morning. She slumbered in her chair in the living room while others watched the Vietnamese evening news on TV. She rarely paid attention to the news or events happening around her, especially not what was happening on the battlefield almost 100 miles from home. A few of my friends from church had heard I was missing in action from an American missionary who happened to have contact with my unit. But none of them wanted to bring the terrible news to my parents. Furthermore, the ARVN failed to notify my parents of my status. Apparently MIA notifications took a back seat since there were too many casualties to process from the battlefront.

That evening the whole family gathered for the regular weekly evening family prayer time. We sang hymns. My father opened the Bible and read from Psalm 91:

> *Those who live in the shelter of the Most High*
> *will find rest in the shadow of the Almighty.*
>
> *He alone is my refuge, my place of safety;*
> *he is my God, and I am trusting him.*

He will shield you with his wings.
He will shelter you with his feathers.
His faithful promises are your armor and protection.

Do not be afraid of the terrors of the night,
nor fear the dangers of the day.

Though a thousand fall at your side,
though ten thousand are dying around you,
these evils will not touch you.

For he orders his angels to protect you wherever you go.
They will hold you with their hands
to keep you from striking your foot on a stone.

The Lord says, "I will rescue those who love me.
I will protect those who trust in my name."

(excerpts from Psalm 91, NLT)

– CHAPTER 13 –

The Battle of An Loc

On the morning of April 13, less than 24 hours after Maj. Davidson and I were airlifted from An Loc, the NVA launched a massive attack with tanks and a large infantry force to take the besieged city. It was the beginning of what historians called "the single most decisive battle in the Vietnam War."

As news that the fighting in An Loc became more ferocious each day, I was concerned for many of my friends stationed there. I cut short my vacation and went to Bien Hoa where Advisory Team 47 had set up a temporary office.

I met Maj. Robert Blair and Mr. Robert Rice, the Deputy Province Senior Advisor of Advisory Team 47, at the team office in Bien Hoa. They both told me the situation in An Loc was becoming increasingly grim. Flights in and out of An Loc were suspended indefinitely. I asked if there was any possibility I could return. Mr. Rice told me that a decision from the higher command was that I was not allowed to return to An Loc any time soon. I asked for a reason, and he said I had suffered enough through my ordeal. So I just hung around in the office for the next two months, monitoring the battle from a distance.

I was amazed by the ferocity of the fighting in An Loc. Never in the history of war had such a small piece of land come under such an explosive force. The NVA deployed 36,000 troops, including tanks and heavy artillery units, to attack the 6,000 defenders which consisted of the 5th ARVN Infantry Division, RF soldiers and the three battalions of the 3rd Ranger Group, including a dozen U.S. advisors who were ordered to stay with their Vietnamese counterparts.

At six o'clock in the morning on April 13, the NVA launched ground assaults with two infantry regiments, T54 tanks and PT76 amphibious tanks in support. Within minutes, one of the columns of tanks punched into the heart of the city. At first the defenders were all shaken and disarrayed. None of them had ever seen any enemy tanks in all their lives. However, the enemy tank column had moved too fast and their infantry support had fallen behind. Some of the enemy tanks had their hatches open with the gunmen standing on top as if they were in a parade, apparently assuming the city had been liberated. Soon a RF soldier named Binh Doan Quang took out his M72 Light Anti-tank Weapon (LAW) to confront the fearful enemy armor column. He opened fire at the engine compartment of the lead tank and crippled it. Instantly word spread and the defenders' morale lifted. Some even climbed up the crippled enemy tank, opened the hatch and dropped in a grenade. In one case at the southern defensive perimeter when a T54 tank broke into their defensive position, an ARVN artillery unit lowered its 105mm howitzer and fired directly onto it and destroyed it.[1]

Meanwhile, QL-13 was entirely cut off by elements of the 7th NVA Division, denying any reinforcement and resupply by ground from the south to the besieged city. The defenders only relied on air support to defend their now crumbling city.

The situation in the city rapidly deteriorated, and on April 16 the 81st ARVN Airborne Ranger Group was airlifted from central Vietnam to An Loc. I always admired this group of the elite special force soldiers. They were young and experienced. Unlike any other regular ARVN units, these brave soldiers usually operated in small cells behind enemy lines to conduct secret reconnaissance operations. This time they were injected into the northern section of the besieged city to root out heavily-armed and well-entrenched enemy pockets. During the next two nights, under cover of darkness, these special force soldiers inched their way into the enemy positions to launch surprise attacks. Sgt. 1st Class Jesse Yearta, Light Weapons Advisor to the 81st Rangers, accompanied an assault squad and directed the Spectre's fire in the form of a rolling barrage in order that the AC-130s fire control officer would be able to keep the ordnance right in front of the friendly troops.[1] As a result, they took back the city one block at a time. After a fierce firefight, they finally cleared out the enemy positions. Again, on April 18, the enemy attacks were more intense with more tanks and, again, they were driven back.

Every day — with constant, heavy rocket and artillery shelling between 1,200 to 2,000 rounds, and repeat ground attacks — the siege had taken a toll on the defenders.[2] There was enough medical treatment for minor wounds. However, the severely wounded ones never made it.

On May 9, based on the previous attack pattern of heavy bombardment followed by major ground assault and with intelligence from captured NVA prisoners, Maj. Gen. James H. Hollingsworth anticipated such an attack was imminent. He redirected all U.S. air power in Southeast Asia at that time, including 170 B52 Stratofortress bombers. He plotted grid boxes around the city the size of 1 km. wide by 3 km. long and assigned each box a number so that the defenders could call at any time.[3]

As anticipated on the morning of May 11, the NVA bombardment dramatically increased. For the next four hours, more than 8,000 rounds of artillery and rockets fell onto the ARVN defensive positions that now had shrunk to only 1000 yards by 1800 yards. The intensity was far more than anyone could imagine. It was equivalent to about five bombs per second and ten rounds per square yard. In such heavy barrage, anyone venturing outside of their fortified bunkers would face certain death.

At 5:30 in the morning, two columns of enemy tank spearheaded from the northeast and west punched into the city with massive infantry units marching from behind. This time the defenders were ready to deal a significant blow to the attackers from a high altitude position. For the next 30 hours straight, and for every 55 minutes, the defenders guided each B52 Arclight cell (three aircrafts) to pre-designated target boxes to smash the enemy's attacking elements. Some of the bombs landed as close as 500 yards from the friendly defensive positions.[3] Never in the history of warfare had such destructive fire power been so concentrated in a small area and within a short period. At the end, the NVA had suffered heavy casualties and withdrew.

For the next two days, the NVA launched more ground attacks into the city, but with much less intensity. Again they were driven out. After several failed attempts to take An Loc, the enemy redirected their effort to cut off reinforcements and supplies to the defenders and continued to bombard the city that was already in ruin. By mid-June, the once powerful NVA force had suffered more than 10,000 deaths and 15,000 wounded. They finally retreated into the jungle officially ending the so-called Nguyen Hue (Easter) Offensive.[3]

Civilians who were trapped inside the city also suffered heavy loss. Many of them took shelter in houses that were not able to sustain the heavy bombardment. They either ended up being killed or buried alive in their own homes. An Loc Hospital, the only medical facility in town, overflowed with the dead and injured. It was shelled repeatedly and the Red Cross marking was all but obliterated by enemy shrapnel. An enemy shell blew up the hospital morgue, hurling corpses into the air. One mass grave of dead from the hospital was stacked with more than 600 bodies, including those of many unclaimed children.

Early in May, in a single night, more than 500 civilians were killed or injured.[4]

At that time, thousands of horrified refugees poured into Phu Cuong, the provincial capital of Binh Duong province 30 miles north of Saigon. The government set up a large camp at the Phu Cuong high school soccer field to accommodate the refugees. Eventually Advisory Team 47 relocated to Phu Cuong so that we could closely monitor the refugee situation and provide any possible help to them. I spent the next ten months working between the refugee camp and the Advisory Team office.

I heard many horror stories of their escape in the camp. At the beginning of the offensive, these refugees risked running into the enemy blockade as they fled south to Chon Thanh. Eventually the South Vietnamese government provided transportation to bring them to the refugee camp. However, many were not so lucky and were trapped amidst the fighting. They were fired upon by the NVA when they tried to escape from the besieged city.

One common plight was that the NVA would capture able men or women from 20 to 40 years of age to work as laborers for their troops. They were forced to transport ammunition and food supplies to their fighters in the frontline. I met a man named Huynh Van Lam who told me he was forced to collect dead NVA corpses in the battlefield and carry them back to a burial site near Can Lo Creek (north of An Loc). He also described how he saw decomposed corpses in a line more than a mile long alongside a trail in the jungle. His group of "laborers" worked day and night, yet they still could not keep up with the burial work. Lam eventually escaped during an air-raid at night. He found his way to the refugee camp.

One morning as I worked with the medical team in the center courtyard of the refugee camp, I saw Maj. Thinh (the former Loc Ninh district chief) walk in. He was surprised to see me there. After a short conversation, I asked him about what happened to Capt. Wanat and the rest of the team after we were ambushed and separated on QL-13 the first night of our escape. Even I had received word that Capt. Wanat was captured 31 days later by a NVA patrol near Can Le Bridge, but I wanted to hear from Maj. Thinh myself what exactly had happened.

"You see, at the moment we were ambushed," Maj Thinh explained, "my body guards were either killed or vanished. Luckily Wanat and I got away without injury. We hid in the jungle for a couple of days and eventually found our way to a montagnard hamlet. There was a family in the hamlet I knew who willingly sheltered us. One day I ventured outside of the house and found my way to An Loc."

"So you left Wanat behind?"

"Tinh, honestly, I had no other choice. The NVA was everywhere. I barely made it out by myself," he tried to explain to me.

"No offense, sir, but that doesn't justify what you did to him. You do not abandon your friend who speaks no Vietnamese and has no knowledge about the territory in a montagnard hamlet!" I was getting furious, almost screaming at him.

"Tinh, you don't understand. No one would accompany a tall American in my situation!" he explained. I walked away without saying another word, and I never spoke to him again.

I was disappointed at his cowardly conduct and selfishness but, at the same time, I also understood his argument, whether justifiable or not. Some of my friends had criticized me for being so naïve in creeping through enemy territory with Maj. Davidson. I never would take any credit that I led Maj. Davidson to safety. In fact, I am glad we did not have to go through the ordeal alone. If I were in his situation, I would want someone to help me get out of the hostile, foreign territory.

Since the fighting kept me from returning to An Loc anytime soon,

I decided to enroll in the College of Liberal Arts at Saigon University for a major in literature. I attended classes as much as my unit allowed, and sometimes I went AWOL to keep up with the class requirements. Life is short, I told myself. I needed to prepare myself to face the challenges ahead whenever this war ended.

CHAPTER 14

Cease Fire

Despite defeat in An Loc, the North Vietnamese were still unwilling to negotiate seriously in the Paris peace talks. On December 18, 1972, the U.S. launched a major air campaign against targets in North Vietnam. The 11-day campaign was dubbed "Operation Linebacker II," also known as the "Christmas Bombings." The bombing was so intense that China had to open its borders to allow North Vietnamese civilians and government officials to take refuge. At that time, I talked to a few colleagues who worked in the intelligence field. They speculated that if the relentless bombings continued for three more days, the North Vietnamese government would have to surrender. The bombing ended on December 29. Finally, the air campaign had driven the North Vietnamese negotiators back to the table.

On January 27, 1973, the Paris Treaty was established to end the war. It was signed by U.S. Secretary of State William Rogers and North Vietnamese Foreign Minister Le Duc Tho at the protest of South Vietnamese President Nguyen Van Thieu due to many unacceptable terms imposed on South Vietnam. The treaty did not require the withdrawal of 125,000 to 145,000 NVA from South Vietnam.

The cease fire was to take effect at midnight January 27, 1973.

I arrived at the Advisory Team office in Phu Cuong on the morning of the day the cease fire was to take effect. I was shocked to learn

Lt. Col. William B. Nolde of Michigan, who replaced Lt. Col. Robert Corley as senior advisor to Binh Long province, was killed in An Loc overnight. An enemy artillery shell slammed into the sandbag wall near the entrance of the TOC bunker where he stayed. He died just eleven hours before the cease fire went into effect. He was the last American soldier to die in combat in the Vietnam War.

The whole team was saddened and shaken by the news. Though I only worked with Lt. Col. Nolde when he returned to the Advisory Team office in Phu Cuong, I traveled with him to visit refugee camps and hospitals. I admired him because of his compassion for the refugees who escaped from An Loc to Phu Cuong. He told me his desire was that someday he would return to a peaceful Vietnam and help rebuild the city of An Loc from the ruins. Sadly, his dream was shattered only moments before the guns were silenced.

By the end of March 1973, all U.S. military forces withdrew from Vietnam and I returned to An Loc to wait for my new assignment. On April 3, I took an ARVN Chinook helicopter to the besieged city and landed at the same soccer field where I was evacuated almost a year earlier. I was saddened to see the devastation the fighting had caused. The city was littered with piles of rubble and unexploded ordnances. Most of the buildings and houses were destroyed, covered with overgrown weeds as tall as a grown man. Many crippled NVA T54 and PT76 tanks lay strewn across the landscape, graffiti tagged on their rusted gun turrets. There were more graves in the city than living souls. Besides the few marked cemeteries honoring those who had sacrificed their lives, there were many unmarked mass graves for the rest of the dead. Friendly and enemy soldiers alike were buried in the same grave. Even a year later people still found remains scattered in the woods outside the city limits.

Despite the cease fire, sporadic shelling continued. The majority of combat deaths in An Loc during this period were caused by incoming enemy rockets or mortars fired randomly day or night, without any warning, into our positions. This made daily chores above ground extremely dangerous. Nevertheless, no one wanted to live like a rat. I tried to make life as normal as possible even though I no longer had any concept of normalcy. I developed the instinct of recognizing the sound of incoming enemy fire from a distance that allowed me enough time to run for cover. Every time I saw someone suddenly running, chances were a rocket or artillery shell was about to hit. I'd either run for cover, or drop to the ground immediately.

Aside from random shells that would fall in the ruins of An Loc, life moved at a more relaxed pace. I set up my cot in the underground communication bunker with five other friends who, like me, were waiting for another assignment. Each morning, we reported to the S1 (personnel office) for daily chores but, for most of the time, we had the whole day free for ourselves. We set up a small "kitchen" of two stoves on top of the bunker furnished with a table and a few chairs made out of ammunition boxes. Every afternoon we walked to a creek nearby to bathe and to bring back water for cooking. On the way, we picked up fresh vegetable from a garden farm.

One of my friends came up with a brilliant idea. He rummaged through the rubble and gathered some large pots and pans, as well as a few scraps of aluminum pipes. He located an abandoned house outside the camp with part of the roof still intact. Soon he started a makeshift distillery for making Vietnamese rice wine, a commodity that was in high demand on this isolated military post. Every day I helped him collect fire wood and carry rice and water to his impromptu wine distillery. It was an excellent way to supplement my mediocre military pay.

Outside my bunker was a large sycamore tree. I made a hammock out of a red U.S. mail bag and tied it up between the tree and a supporting pole of the roof of the bunker. It became my little sanctuary in the middle of this ruined war zone. Each day I spent some of my free time there reading, studying and even dozing off under the cool shade. It was only a few steps from the bunker's entrance in case I needed to run for cover.

One morning as I was lying on the hammock reading my daily devotion, my colleague Sgt. Le Hoang Tam asked me to follow him to the bunker. He wanted to show me a new gadget he had brought back from his recent trip to Saigon. As we reached the bottom of the stairs of the bunker, suddenly a massive explosion shook the whole place. Dust and choking smoke darkened the room. The sandbag roof covering the entrance caved in, sending a ton of sandbags down the stairway. However, the concrete stairs were still intact. A few minutes later I went outside to find that the top of the sycamore tree was totally gone and my red, homemade hammock was shred to pieces. The rope of the hammock still dangled loosely on the tree trunk. Next to it was a large crater at least a foot deep, and in the bottom of the crater was a 122mm rocket tailpiece. If I had waited 30 seconds to follow Sgt. Tam into the bunker, I would have suffered the same fate as my poor homemade hammock.

It did not take very long before I located the apartment where I used to stay. A large bomb crater sprawled over the once beautiful front lawn. All that was left of the single-story building was a crumbled cement slab. From the rubble, I found a Chinese New Testament Bible I used to own. It was covered with mold, but the pages were still intact. It was the only item I recovered from my apartment.

One afternoon as I wandered around the graveyard near the old marketplace I found a tombstone simply marked with red ink: "Sergeant First Class Nguyen Cong Son. 1945-1972."

Son was a close friend of mine. We had both served together as interpreters for Advisory Team 47. His fiancée Miss Cuc, tall and beautiful, was a civilian secretary at the MACCORDS office in An

Loc where I worked. Her father was an ARVN 1st Lieutenant serving with the Regional Force in An Loc district. Son and Cuc got engaged long before the battle of An Loc started. They had planned their wedding for the month of May that year. However, as fighting erupted in April, Son had to stay in An Loc. Cuc escaped with her family from the besieged city and arrived at Phu Cuong refugee camp in late April. Unfortunately, her father was killed in the battle of An Loc. By the end of June 1972, as the fighting in An Loc gradually subsided, Son supposedly took a week of vacation to fly to Phu Cuong to marry Cuc. Everything had been planned well. The wedding ceremony took place in a Catholic church, followed by a simple dinner at the refugee camp, and I was invited.

On July 9, as Son was waiting at the soccer field for a flight out of An Loc, a rocket struck where he was standing, killing him instantly. I was devastated by the news. On the same day, I received terrible news from Cuc's family that she had passed out and was admitted to the hospital.

I went to the hospital on my lunchbreak that afternoon. Walking into the inpatient ward, I saw Cuc curled up on a hospital bed with both hands covering her face. She seemed to be sleeping peacefully. I sat silently in a chair and waited. This poor girl had been through too much. She had lost her father a few months back and now, as a newlywed bride, she was a widow!

She woke up to see me sitting by her bed. She started crying hysterically, "Tinh, Why? Why?!" she looked at me through swollen eyes and held my hands, as if I had the answer to all her troubles.

I tried to console her, but I could not even speak a word of comfort. I tried to grieve with her, but I had no tears to shed. I sat there like a statue with no response and no feeling. Suddenly, for the first time, I realized I had lost my ability to express any emotions, needless to say, to comfort a broken heart and a shattered soul.

I felt devastated and horrified. How could I turn into such a person who had lost the ability to express his feelings? Instead of returning to work that afternoon, I strolled along the bank of the Saigon River near the Advisory Team compound to do some soul-searching. Six years of fighting on the battlefield had desensitized me to a point that I was no longer able to respond to emotion. Yes, I had to control my inner self, overcome fear, get rid of anxiety, and be brave in accepting death in order to survive. I was indoctrinated to hate my enemy before I could pull the trigger. I had to suppress my feelings in order to cope with the loss of friends no matter how much pain I felt. Was this change permanent? How much had it affected my behavior?

It was no wonder some of my friends said I was a changed person. I was rude to them and my anger had driven them away from me. I felt as if I was trapped inside a cage of violence. Even if I could break away, there was no place I could go to escape the reality of war. Bombs continued to drop and bullets still cut through the air in spite of the peace treaty. Dying and wailing continued and there was no end in sight! The scars of war had wounded again and again, so deeply, rotting the core of my soul. Where was my healing?

My struggle continued for many years even after the war ended. Not only did I have to deal with the resentment of defeat, suppressing my anger and fear, but I also tried to erase the horrors of war from my memories. In this long and painful process of seeking to become "normal" again, I found myself spending more time studying the source of all healing: Scriptures — the Word of God. I came to the conclusion that healing must begin by making peace with God, and then I can be at peace with myself, and finally, live in peace with others.

After three months of hanging around the ruins of An Loc, I received transfer orders to the ARVN Signal Corps. My technical training would begin once I reported to the Army Signal School in Vung Tau.

July 10, 1973, I stood at the now famous soccer field and waited for the flight out of An Loc. I looked around the familiar landscape for the last time. There were so many memories I had held dear to me. This beloved city had changed so much. The once vibrant rubber planta-tion town of more than 20,000 had enjoyed security and economic prosperity when the U.S. and ARVN forces were stationed here. Now all had crumbled into ruin. The once robust marketplace down the street became a mass graveyard. The high school grounds became no man's land. The shouting and screaming of the soccer match on the field was now silent. So many of my friends had died and were buried in the graves nearby. Many who had survived the ordeal vowed never to return. They had suffered enough and seen more misery than they could bear. As for me, I had invested three years of my life in An Loc in hopes that one day this city could see normalcy, but now it was all up in the air. Nevertheless, the city of An Loc, a symbol of the South Vietnamese' will to stand against the North Vietnamese invasion, was etched deep into my memory. There was no way I could forget this city, no matter how hard I tried.

I began Signal Corps training at Vung Tau Signal Training Center and specialized in field communication and telephone switchboard repairs. All my classmates were friends who had also served as inter-preters in the armed service.

Vung Tau, 50 miles southeast of Saigon, was a resort town with beautiful beaches, nice hotels and gourmet restaurants. It had only known peace, and there were hardly any scars of the war around. It used to be an R&R resort for American GIs, a far cry from the battle-scarred city of An Loc.

For me, it was a long-overdue retreat. It gave me time to relax and recuperate from the exhaustion of the battlefield and provided a sense of normalcy away from the war. My studies in the training center were not intense at all. Our daily routine was eight hours of class and lab each day, plus guard duty every other night. Each weekend we had passes to go home or go to the beach. Every Wednesday evening the camp granted the whole squad a two-hour pass to go grocery shopping or to the bars nearby for a drink. The only requirement was that we had to return as a group before the gate closed at nine o'clock.

Most of my friends in the unit called me "*Muc Su* (Pastor) Tinh" because I neither drank nor smoked and I went to chapel every Sunday. In spite of all their teasing we got along well. Very often they came to me for advice when they ran into family or marital issues. My assignment on every Wednesday evening was to pick up groceries for the whole squad while the others enjoyed happy hour in the bars. I did not mind my task at all.

One evening after I picked up the groceries, I came to the bar where most of my friends were hanging around. As I sat at a corner waiting, a young girl in her twenties came over and threw her arms around me. Then she started fondling and kissing me, and asked me to go to bed with her. I was so embarrassed while everyone in the bar was laughing and cheering, clapping and pounding the tables. As I was trying to break away from her, the girl suddenly screamed "*Troi Oi!* (Oh heaven!) I can't see! I can't see!" She covered her face with her hands and bustled out of the bar. Now everyone was startled and staring at me as if had done something to her. I knew that I didn't do anything improper. There was no smoke of any kind in the room and yet she was the only one being affected by it. A few minutes later when she walked back into the bar, her teary eyes were swollen and red. This time she stayed behind the counter looking warily in my direction.

I left the bar with my friends wondering what really happened. A few days later, my friends admitted they had chipped in to bet that if any girl could seduce me she would get pay plus a double bonus. I believe that the Lord had protected me from the temptations of sexual immorality. From then on, they would not play tricks on me again.

Although the Peace Treaty had been signed, the fighting continued. In 1973 alone, the ARVN suffered more than 25,000 deaths in combat, exceeding any of the previous years except for 1968 (the year of the Tet Offensive) and 1972 (the year of the Easter Offensive). From the beginning, many of us doubted the legitimacy of the peace treaty. To us it seemed the Americans wanted to pull out of Vietnam, no matter the cost, and wanted nothing to do with the war anymore. The NVA needed time to regroup and refit their battered divisions after their Easter Offensive defeat. As for the South Vietnamese, well, they were doomed even before the ink on the Peace Treaty had dried. For each blatant violation of the treaty by the NVA, the U.S. neither protested nor retaliated. The promised support by the U.S. never materialized, leaving the South Vietnamese government fighting a poor man's war by themselves.

In August 1974, President Richard Nixon resigned in disgrace after the Watergate scandal. Early in December, the NVA launched a coordinated attack with armored and infantry divisions on Phuc Binh city, the provincial capital of Phuoc Long Province, 75 miles northeast of Saigon. Within days the province fell into the enemy's hands. Lieutenant Colonel Nguyen Thong Thanh, the province chief, was killed along with his family members in the provincial headquarters. I worked with LTC Thanh when he was deputy military commander of Binh Long Province. He was an assistant to Col. Nhut during the siege of An Loc. The loss of a province, though not considered as strategically important as An Loc, drew no response from the U.S. despite repeated protests by the South Vietnamese Government. I sensed something terrible was going to happen soon.

Two months later, the Democrat-controlled U.S. Congress voted to totally cut off all military funding to the South Vietnamese government and suspended all U.S. military activities in Southeast Asia, leaving the ill-equipped ARVN force to face the onslaught of the well-equipped, refreshed North Vietnamese Army.

In January 1974, after four months of technical training at the ARVN Signal School in Vung Tau, I received my transfer to the 654th Signal Battalion stationed in Bien Hoa. Instead of doing technical work that I had been trained for, they assigned me to the battalion headquarters S5 Political and Psychological warfare unit.

One day I got a call to the S1 (personnel) office. The sergeant in charge told me that many details of my military record were missing. It only showed that I was an administrative clerk since the first day I joined the ARVN. Nothing indicated that I worked for the U.S. advisory team as a military interpreter for the past seven years, and all of the combat decorations I had earned were nowhere to be found in my file. It was not even updated since the day I began to work with the U.S. advisory team, which meant a highly unusual mistake had been made. I was furious for the omissions, as they probably cost me a promotion and pay raise. Nevertheless, the sergeant told me that he would take time to correct the errors for me.

Sometimes we see things that happen in life as a curse, but often they turn out to be blessings in disguise. The errors in my military record might have cost me a promotion, but would eventually save my life.

CHAPTER 15

The Fall of Saigon

Early in February, 1975, I received orders to attend a three-month training course at the Political Warfare School in the Capital Special Zone Headquarters in Saigon, a required course for my position as a political warfare specialist.

I did not expect the situation to change so rapidly within one short month. On March 10, 1975, while I was still attending Political Warfare School, the NVA launched a major offensive in Central Highland. Within days the NVA captured Ban Me Thuot and six other provinces. South Vietnam was cut in half. ARVN soldiers and civilians retreated in disarray. The NVA also captured Quang Tri, Da Nang, and other provinces in central Vietnam while the ARVN only put up token resistance. And soon the NVA had advanced into the capital city of Saigon.

On April 21, President Nguyen Van Thieu resigned, handing over the now crumbling nation to his successor Tran Van Huong. He fled to Taiwan with his family, allegedly taking suitcases of bullion gold bars belonging to the Treasury Department of the South Vietnamese government. As the situation turned from bad to worse, I realized the country would sooner or later fall into the hands of the NVA. I was certain that my life was in danger if I stayed and decided to look for a way to leave the country as soon as possible.

Every afternoon after class I would go to the U.S. embassy in Saigon and look for passage to leave the country. I showed my decorations and documents, including my Silver Star medal, to the Marine guards at the embassy gate and begged for permission to plead my case to the embassy personnel inside. They denied me every time I tried. I did this every day for more than a week, until one day the guards threatened to shoot me if I refused to stay away. I stood across the street from the embassy and watched helplessly as busloads of people, some dressed like bar girls, headed for Tan Son Nhut International airport for an evacuation flight out of the country. I felt betrayed and disgusted.

One evening I went to see my longtime friend Mr. Cuong Ha. Mr. Ha worked for a U.S. civil agency in Saigon. I shared with him my frustration and my urgency to get out of the country by any means.

"How much money do you have?" Cuong asked.

"What do you mean how much money do I have?" I did not understand his question.

Then he told me that two days earlier he arranged for a Vietnamese family of four to get on the evacuation flight through his U.S. embassy connection. The cost was one million piaster (equivalent to 4,000 U.S. dollars at current black market rate), and he guaranteed success. If I had enough cash he would do me a favor by not charging me his share of commission.

I told him I would not be able to raise that large amount of cash in such a short time. At the very least I could scrounge up a few hundred U.S. dollars. He said he would see what he could do for me.

I had little hope for his arrangement, but this was not an isolated case at all. I witnessed or heard of many similar under-the-table deals like this that took place in the days leading up to the fall of Saigon. Nevertheless, corruption is like a plague. It could infiltrate every level and affect everyone, Vietnamese and Americans alike. Even the U.S. embassy officials were not immune to it. They, too, wanted to pocket a few more bucks one last time before packing up and leaving town.

On the afternoon of April 28 I went to the U.S. Defense Attaché's Office next to Tan Son Nhut Airport in the hope that I could somehow take a flight out. There were a few hundred people packed at the entrance. The Marine guard did not know what to do. It was chaotic. After a few hours of fruitless attempts, I gave up and went home. At six o'clock in the evening the NVA started shelling the airport and the outskirts of the capital with mortars and rockets. The capital authority declared a state of emergency and enforced a 24-hour curfew. The NVA had advanced to Biet Hoa, 25 miles northeast of Saigon.

The next morning, April 29, people ventured outside disregarding the curfew law. The local police no longer enforced the curfew and some even abandoned their stations. Looters started ransacking government buildings and police stations. The villa that once belonged to Gen. Cao Van Vien, Chairman of the Joint Chiefs of Staff of ARVN, located in a cul-de-sac of Cho Lon, was no exception. Looters dragged TVs, furniture and appliances out onto the street. ARVN soldiers and policeman took off their uniforms and mingled with local residents. Some hitchhiked or begged others to take them home. They had all given up before the enemy entered the capital. Lawlessness plunged the city into chaos and fear.

There was no reason to go to class that day, and I assumed everyone in the Political Warfare School had also fled. Early in the afternoon, as I stood at a street corner chatting with a friend, I saw a crippled ARVN C130 military transport plane crash into an abandoned hotel on Ngo Quyen Street in downtown Cho Lon. Apparently, it was shot down by anti-aircraft fire. The impact and explosion shook the entire neighborhood and shattered the glass windows of houses a few blocks away. Smoke filled several street blocks nearby, yet no fire engines showed up to extinguish the fire. The next day I walked by the crash site. There were charred bodies still scattered on the street or dangling from the hotel windows. A few scavengers wandered around the smoldering building to search for valuable belongings.

In the afternoon I went to the U.S. embassy again for one last attempt to get out. A friend of mine drove me through the partly barricaded streets in Cho Lon to the downtown square on Ngyuen Hue Street. Once crowded shopping malls were now closed. The streets were deserted except for a few dead bodies lying near a statue in the center of Nam Son Square. No one had bothered to remove them. As I approached the embassy, hundreds of people were gathered outside the main gate and other high rises nearby. It was complete chaos. The crowd blocked the entrance. Men and women clung to the fence wall trying to get inside the embassy compound as the Marine guards pushed them back. I tried to get close to the gate and was pushed back by the crowd. I assumed many were just like me who had affiliation with the Americans. They, too, tried desperately to get out and were frightened as if the world was coming to an end.

Inside the compound the situation was not any better. The fortunate ones still had to wait in line where hundreds already lined the stairs leading to the helipad on the roof of the embassy. Every 20 to 30 minutes a Huey helicopter would land on the rooftop, and pick up only eight to ten people on each run. I went to another high-rise building a few blocks away and the situation was the same. Crowds tried to get inside, the guards pushed them back out. I figured it might take another day before the people already in the compound could be evacuated. Given the fact that the enemy had Saigon surrounded, it was only a matter of hours before they would march to the center of the city without resistance. There was not much hope to waiting on the outside of the embassy.

That evening I returned to Luong Nhu Hoc Christian Church where I usually stayed overnight. I met Mr. Chan A Nguyen who came to seek permission to stay at the church. He felt it was not safe for him to be home alone. Chan A was in his late sixties, a retired major general of the Republic of China (Taiwan) as well as of ARVN. He was a descendent of the famous nineteenth century Vietnamese hero Nguyen Thien Thuat. In the early 1940s, as an ambitious young man, Chan A went to mainland China to study at Whampoa Military Academy. He fought alongside Cheng Kai Shekh's army against the Japanese invasion during WWII and later against the Chinese Communist Army. In October 1949, when the Communists took over China, he retreated to Formosa (currently Taiwan) with Cheng's army. After 25 years of military service in Taiwan, he retired in 1965. Instead of enjoying his retirement years in Taiwan with a hefty pension, he volunteered to return to Vietnam, his native homeland, to fight another war. He was given the rank of major general in the ARVN and served as military advisor at the Psychological Warfare Headquarters in Saigon. He finally retired from his military career in 1972.

One day Chan A's friend invited him to the Luong Nhu Hoc Christian Church, and soon he committed his life to Jesus and was actively involved in the church's ministries. He lived in a government-subsidized villa near the church. His wife moved to Hong Kong to stay with their children. His only relative in town was a distant nephew who lived down the street from the church.

I prepared a bed for Mr. Chan A in a room that the church used as a printing shop. That evening the NVA continued shelling the outskirts of the city as a few low-flying helicopters zipped through the dark sky for the last chance to get out. The streets were all deserted.

It was a sleepless night for both of us. I was nervous, wondering what would happen the next morning when the NVA marched into the city of Saigon. What would they do with thousands of South Vietnamese government officials and soldiers like me? Chan A insisted that he never intended to surrender.

"I am a professional soldier. For all my life, I shed blood on the battlefield to defend freedom. I'd rather die instead of surrender to the communists I have fought against all my life."

"Then, why didn't you leave the country sooner since you had so many connections?" I asked curiously.

"Well, it is a long story," he said. "Two weeks ago as the situation deteriorated, I went to the Taiwanese Embassy. Since I was the former high ranking military officer of the Republic of China, Ambassador Hsu Shau Tseng was my subordinate during the years he served in the Taiwanese army. He assured me the embassy had reserved a seat for me on an evacuation flight chartered by the Taiwanese Government. He even told me to relax and wait in the comfort of my home and that his staff would come to get me when my flight arrived. I waited for one week, but no one came. Finally, I went to the embassy myself two days ago to find it was vacated and the gate locked and chained. Later, someone told me the embassy had sold my seat to someone who paid a hefty price for it. I was so angry and felt betrayed."

"What are you going to do now?"

"Tomorrow I'll leave for Can-Tho (a city in the southern delta region) to see a friend in the hope that he can help me."

I felt sorry for him and found we had more in common. He and I both were abandoned by those we had faithfully served for many years. Though he was a general and I had my ties to the American military, we both would soon face the same fate at the hands of our enemy.

The next morning, April 30, 1975, the street was unusually crowded. Everyone roamed around waiting to see what was going to happen next. By 10:30 a.m., Duong Van Minh (Big Minh), who was president for only three days, announced on the national radio that all South Vietnamese forces were to lay down their arms, cease hostilities, and stay where they were. He also invited the Viet Cong Provisional Revolutionary Government to engage in a ceremony of orderly transfer of power so as to avoid further bloodshed to the population. It was obvious that the North Vietnamese had no intention of any compromise. Instead, they marched into the city as conquerors. The leading NVA tanks crashed through the gates of the Independence Palace. They arrested Duong Van Minh and his staff. Soon the National Liberation Front flag was raised over the Palace. Later in the afternoon, Minh announced on the radio that the South Vietnamese Government had completely dissolved, officially ending the Vietnam War.[1]

As soon as I heard the news on the radio, I hurried home to find my mother stooped by a wood stove. She was burning my military uniforms, documents and pictures, including the Silver Star Medal and Army Commendation Medal I earned from the U.S. military — everything that had to do with my military service. She was anxious and her hands were shaking as she placed each item onto the fire.

She looked up and saw me standing next to her. She said, "Tinh, I need to get rid of these things. I am worrying what they (the VC) will do to you if these fall into their hands!"

"Mom, that is OK. These items don't do any good anymore. God will take care of me." I tried to comfort her as I watched the proof of my glory turning into ash.

I never boasted about my military achievement to anyone. I always kept a low profile and seldom put on my uniform when I returned home from leave. Even some of my neighbors had no idea that I served in the military. My parents had a respectable reputation in our small neighborhood and most of our neighbors were my close childhood friends. Unless someone intended to betray me for whatever reason, or allegedly report me to the new regime, I would have less trouble staying in this neighborhood until I could find a way to leave the country.

The next morning, May 1, I went to see a friend who told me the day before that he might be able to get me on a boat to leave the country. When I arrived, he said his contact had to scrap the plan because the NVA had taken control of the seaport. We decided to take a ride to Saigon to see what was going on in the capital a day after the "liberation."

Some stores on both sides of Dong Khanh Street and Tran Hung Dao Street, the main artery connecting Cho Lon and Saigon, were finally open for business. Restaurants were packed and tables spilled over onto the sidewalk. Police or security was nowhere in sight except for several NVA soldiers dressed in green uniforms, pith helmets, and tire-rubber sandals who were standing guard at some main street corners.

As we approached the downtown square, many Soviet-made tanks and military vehicles were lined along the streets. The Independence Palace, the symbol of the power of the South Vietnamese Government, was intact except for the main gate which had turned into a pile of mangled steel on the ground. A red and blue flag with a yellow star was flying high under the hot, morning sun. A large banner hung on the fence saying "Nothing is more precious than independence and freedom." On the street outside the palace, hundreds of curious onlookers mingled with the soldiers as if the circus had come to town. I joined a group listening to an old NVA soldier (who looked like a hillbilly to me) brag about how his unit had defeated the mighty army of American imperialism and had liberated the South.

One lady standing next to me raised a question, "Can you compare Hanoi to Saigon?"

"Of course, Hanoi is a more modern and beautiful city and we have everything," he continued to brag.

"Do you have that many scooters crowding the street?" She was asking out of curiosity, not intending to start a debate.

"Ah…" he hesitated and looked away as if he had been caught in a lie. "Your people should thank the Party for liberating you from the tyranny of Thieu's puppet regime." He tried to change the subject to avoid digging a bigger hole for himself.

Saigon was a vibrant and modern city despite suffering the wrath brought down on her by the war. While the South Vietnamese enjoyed the protection of basic freedoms similar to other countries in Southeast Asia, North Vietnam was ruled by a communist dictatorial party and was at least 20 years behind the South in terms of modern amenities.

It was ironic, then, how the term "liberation" was used so openly to justify the action of an oppressive, backward power to invade a peaceful, free nation. In no time, North Vietnam imposed the ideology of tyranny to replace the free will of the people. A dark era had descended on the people of South Vietnam.

I came back to the church that evening to find Chan A standing by the gate. He just returned from Can Tho, disappointed that he had missed the boat. His friend had gone two days before he got there. Earlier that day he arrived at his home to find his house confiscated and now occupied by a squad of NVA soldiers. He seemed resigned to the fact that he had exhausted every means to escape. He was too old to run, financially broke and now homeless. The church arranged for him to stay in a church-run orphanage in Phu Lam, a suburb of the city. The next morning I took him there on my motorcycle and promised to come to see him again.

A week later I went to the orphanage to visit Chan A. He was staying in a small room with a bunk bed and an old wooden table placed against the window facing the courtyard. He was happy that I had kept my promise to come to see him.

"Tinh, I want to show you something." He handed me several empty medicine bottles.

"What are these?' I puzzled for a moment.

"Last night I committed suicide." He said as he sat down on the bed "I took a total of 75 sleeping pills" His voice was as strong as ever.

"Seventy five pills, why?" I asked as I tried to decipher the written labels on the bottles.

"I felt it was time for me to go. There was no need to cause trouble for anyone. I would rather die by my own hand than be tortured by the communist regime." He paused for a minute then he pulled out two sealed envelopes from under a pillow on his bed.

"Last night I wrote these two letters, one for the church and one for my nephew." He handed them to me, and then he walked to the table by the window and poured himself a cup of hot tea.

"After I had finished the pills," he continued, "I put on my best three-piece suit and my only pair of leather shoes, and then I went to bed. I assumed that this morning someone would come and wrap me up and bury me without fanfare, the simpler the better. Tinh, I just don't want to bother anyone anymore!" He explained.

I stood holding the empty bottles and the letters he gave me, without saying a word. This poor, old soul truly had nothing to live for except his faith in God.

"Now I know God must have a purpose in this frail, old life," he said as he looked out the window. His voice was as firm and determined as ever, like a fighter ready for another imminent battle.

A week later he reported to the local authority. Soon he was transferred to a labor camp near Hoang Lien Mountain range in North Vietnam where most of the former high ranking military officers and political prisoners were confined. Three months later the church received a letter from him through his nephew. He indicated he was doing well and asked for medication and food supplies. The church collected whatever he requested, and his nephew delivered the supplies to him on his next visit.

In 1987, after 12 years of confinement in the prison camp, Chan A was finally released back to Saigon. (By then I had resettled in the U.S.) From the pictures I received, he was a frail, old man with a well-grown white beard. He proudly proclaimed that he had led many of his prison cellmates, including former Maj. Gen. Nguyen Huu Co, to become followers of Jesus. For him, it was a treasure worth far more than his freedom, and he gladly paid for it with his final years. Six months later, he passed away at the age of 83.

– CHAPTER 16 –

Winners and Losers

On April 30, 1975, as NVA tanks crashed through the gates of the Independence Palace in Saigon, clearly the North Vietnamese Army and its politburo were the winners of the 15-year war. Despite failed offensives and mounting losses, the North Vietnamese found some unexpected friends in the antiwar movement on the streets of America as well as in such radical leftists as Jane Fonda, John Kerry and Walter Cronkite. The North Vietnamese won a psychological victory in Washington D.C. without ever firing a bullet. The American public realized that winning the war was not as easy as what the U.S. government had originally promised. Many felt the cost was too high and demanded U.S. withdrawal from Vietnam. The North Vietnamese politburo realized this and were quite confident their perseverance would eventually pay off and they would win the war. The Paris Peace Treaty that was supposed to bring lasting peace and reconciliation to North and South Vietnam only provided the NVA with badly-needed time to regroup and refit their battered units after their loss of the Easter Offensive and to prepare for the final assault. Their goal of conquering South Vietnam was finally fulfilled in December 1974. When the U.S. Congress decided to cut off all aid to the South Vietnamese government, it was sending a green light signal to the NVA to march freely into Saigon.

Was America defeated by the North Vietnamese Army in the battlefield as some in the media claimed? The answer is absolutely not. When the NVA declared victory in Saigon on April 30, 1975, American military units had already been gone for more than two years. Secondly, contrary to this belief, the NVA was defeated in the battle of An Loc in 1972. During the same year, the U.S. Air Force's massive Christmas Bombings over North Vietnam had pushed the North Vietnamese politburo to the brink of surrender. At the end, in my opinion, the North Vietnamese had won the war with the help of the U.S. antiwar movement on the streets of America.

Undeniably, the NVA defeated the Army of the Republic of Vietnam. The sudden dissolution of a million-man army was unthinkable in modern warfare. Despite their victory at the battle of An Loc, the ARVN had revealed a fault in their ability to fight a conventional war: too much reliance on U.S. military firepower. The rampant corruption and incompetent leadership, from the commander-in-chief to the officers in the battlefield, also contributed to the ARVN's sudden downfall. In the last days of the war, while many soldiers and officers on the battlefield were bravely holding off the enemy's advance, those in the rear had already abandoned their posts and boarded the U.S. evacuation flights out of the country. Many combat officers, including generals, committed suicide instead of surrendering to the enemy.

How did the Vietnamese people see the war? After all, they were the ultimate victims of the 15-year conflict which had cost countless lives both in the north and south. Outside of the figures and estimates of the death toll, stories that I encountered in the aftermath of the war made the true human cost painfully obvious.

Nguyen Van Hai* was a hardworking entrepreneur. He ran a successful auto parts import business on the first floor of a three-story building he owned on Tran Hung Dao Street in Saigon. Hai was born

---

Name has been changed for protection.

in Ha Noi after WWII. In 1954 when Ho Chi Minh and his Viet Minh (Vietnam Independence League, later renamed Vietnam Worker's Party) declared independence from the French colony, Hai left the communist-controlled north and fled to South Vietnam with his parents and younger sister and settled in Saigon. However, his oldest brother Anh* joined the Viet Minh to fight the French, and decided to stay behind.

For more than 20 years the family had totally lost contact with the older brother Anh due to the conflict and did not know whether he was alive or dead. Now that peace had come, the country finally unified. Hai still wondered if he would see his brother again.

Nine months after the fall of Saigon, on a January morning, someone knocked on the door of Hai's now defunct store. He came to open it and, through the steel folding gate, he saw a man in his forties dressed in an untucked white shirt, a greenish pith helmet and a pair of recycled tire sandals. In one hand, he was carrying an old beat-up suitcase and the other a piece of yellow paper.

"Hi, is this the home of Mr. Nguyen Van Hai, son of *Bac* (Uncle) Binh*?" The stranger spoke in North Vietnamese dialect.

"That's me." Hai hesitated for a moment, then asked, "What do you need?"

"I am Anh, your brother. You and I have not seen each other for more than 20 years!"

Hai thought he was dreaming. Standing before him was the long-lost brother he had been thinking about for all of these years. He quickly slid the folding gate open and welcomed him inside. Hai was so excited he called the whole family to come for a reunion feast. Anh was now married and had two children. He was a high-ranking official working for the central government in Hanoi.

During the next ten days, Hai took Anh on a tour of Saigon to visit

---

Name has been changed for protection.

relatives and friends. There was much to talk about after 20 years of separation. However, Anh seemed to avoid talking about life in the North. Hai thought that perhaps it was the nature of people who lived under a restricted society for so long that they were not willing to share their feelings and thoughts with others.

On the evening before Anh returned to Hanoi, they gathered in the living room for a glass of iced tea.

Hai asked his brother "So, what do you think about Saigon?"

"I came to look for you the first time, never expecting you to live in a beautiful house and own a successful business. For all these years I was told by the central government that people in the south are suffering and hungry, under the yoke of American Imperialism. Therefore, the (Vietnamese Worker's) Party and leadership determined to liberate the South from the puppet regime and unify the country."

Anh opened his old, beat-up suitcase and took out a package wrapped in newspaper. He carefully removed the paper and placed the contents on the table — four rice bowls made of clay.

"I brought these bowls as a gift to you," Anh continued, "because they said people in the South have no rice bowls and chopsticks. I feel embarrassed to show them to you now. In fact, you have more than what I could imagine. I don't know what I'm supposed to believe anymore."

Anh took a sip of tea. "Honestly, it's only because you are my brother that I would express these feelings. Here in the city of Saigon I see prosperity and progress. The stores in the Ben Thanh Market are booming. People go about their lives, living in decent houses. It seems everyone owns a motor scooter and some even have automobiles. There is enough food in the market place and you can buy whatever you want so long as you have money to spend. I don't see any sign of the starvation that they had propagated. In the North everything is rationed. Sometimes I blamed it on the war. Fortunately, I am a government official and have more privileges than most ordinary people in the north. Besides, the living conditions in the north are quite different from yours. This is the first time in my life that I've seen that 'thing' in your house."

"What do you mean, that 'thing'?" Hai said, puzzled.

"That thing you have in the outhouse," Anh said, embarrassed.

"Oh, you meant the commode!" Hai reasoned. They both laughed.

Hai leaned on the couch and listened patiently. This was the first time he ever saw his brother share his feelings so candidly.

"Anh," Hai explained, trying not to upset his brother, "we did have a free market society. Everyone could strive to succeed for a better life if they were willing to work hard. In my case, I followed mom and dad to the south when I was a youngster. As I grew older, I worked hard and used my savings to open this auto parts business with the help of banks and friends, and I have become a successful businessman with more than ten employees. Now things have changed for the worse. What you're seeing on the street is the remnant of the past. It will all soon be taken over by the new regime. My business will have to shut down. I have no choice but to lay off everyone. Now I don't know what my future will be like."

Anh quietly listened.

"Yes, I don't deny unification is a good thing." Hai almost lost his composure, forgetting that sitting across the table was a high-ranking communist government official who could arrest him as a reactionary. "However, we don't need your liberation. We've already had the right to exercise our freedom of expression, freedom of religion. I could choose my own career, and invest in whatever business I wanted to invest. I could travel anywhere without restriction from the authorities. Now, everything has changed."

"So do you think the liberation was a mistake?" Anh looked up and asked.

Hai replied without hesitation. "Whether or not it was a mistake is not the point. Most of the people in the south don't care who is running the government, so long as it governs with justice and brings peace to our country. It must allow its citizens the right to choose the form of government and determine the future of our nation without threat and interference by the regime in power. Otherwise, the ultimate losers of the war are the people themselves."

Part Two

The Roaring Sea

"Do not be afraid, for I have ransomed you.
I have called you by name; you are mine.

When you go through deep waters and great trouble,
I will be with you.

When you go through rivers of difficulty,
you will not drown!

When you walk through the fire of oppression,
you will not be burned up; the flames will not consume you.

For I am the Lord, your God,
the Holy One of Israel, your Savior."

Excerpts from Isaiah 43:1-3 (NLT)

– CHAPTER 1 –

Life Under the New Regime

Even as the war had finally come to an end, there was no relief for most of the people in South Vietnam. In April 1975, two weeks prior to the NVA tanks crashing through the gates of the Independence Palace in Saigon, a bloodbath took place in Cambodia. The communist Khmer Rouge government killed 2 million Cambodians. Many feared this could be repeated in Vietnam. Political purging was nothing new to the North Vietnamese Communist government. From 1956-1959, after taking over the North, the communist government launched a "People's Tribunal," putting 200,000 North Vietnamese to death. However, this time a bloodbath had not yet taken place. Perhaps the new regime was still trying to consolidate their control after the sudden collapse of the South Vietnamese government. Also, it would be unwise to do something so horrifying before the watchful eyes of the foreign reporters who remained in Saigon. And they did not want to jeopardize a chance for postwar reconstruction aid which the U.S. had promised to provide under certain articles of the Paris Peace Treaty. However long they waited, though, I knew that sooner or later the new regime would reveal its true cruel intent.

Despite their show of restraint, the "liberators" wasted no time eliminating military and political opposition in the South. Within a week, they ordered all former South Vietnamese government officials, political party members and soldiers to report immediately to the newly-organized provisional local authority. I waited for two days before I reported to the local, temporary office located in an elementary school near my house. An NVA soldier greeted me at the door. He politely asked a few questions before handing me a form. On the form I disclosed my position as an office clerk of the 654th Signal Battalion as indicated on my military record. I turned in the form and he did not ask me any further questions and sent me home.

Two weeks later, another announcement came ordering all former government officials, military officers, and police officers to report to specified assembly sites. The authority instructed them to bring mosquito nets, clothing, personal effects, and enough food for ten days. Many of my friends followed the order, and most assumed it was nothing more than a short course of political indoctrination. They followed the instructions and went. Ten days went by and there was no sign of anyone coming back home. Families who came to inquire about the status of their loved ones were turned away without any information. Soon they realized the government had tricked them into believing it was a short stay. The food supplies they brought were only for a road trip to a "re-education camp." Upon arriving at these camps, they were formally charged as war criminals and required to be "re-educated" in order to be admitted into the "new society." The length of the prison term depended upon how well each prisoner allowed themselves to be brainwashed, how he performed his work, and how he behaved in the camp.

In mid-June 1975, all soldiers, non-commissioned officers and former local officials were ordered to undergo one week of "reform study." I joined many of my neighbors at a local high school gym. The instructor was a young political cadre in his twenties. He paced across the stage, lecturing on how we must be grateful to the Vietnam Labor Party and their hard work in liberating the South Vietnamese from the tyranny of American imperialism. After one week of long hours of indoctrination, we had to write a "confession" of crimes against the Vietnamese people. Obviously, everyone who attended felt it was a joke. Who would accept such a doctrine that was so backward and foolish? Nevertheless, we had no other choice but to write whatever pleased the instructor to get a passing grade. After the indoctrination session they instructed us to stay home and await further assignments. We were not allowed to apply for jobs or travel beyond the city limits without permission.

Meanwhile, my father's textile factory had to shut down due to the new law that all industries were now nationalized. Private businesses would no longer exist. Thus, our family was forced to find another source of income.

On the surface nothing seemed unusual. People went about their lives, buying and selling in market places. Food products were still plentiful but getting expensive. As long as they had cash or gold to spend, one could buy anything on the black market, from Levi® jeans to Yamaha® grand pianos. The rich privately sold their house goods and materials in order to buy gold and foreign currency for their contingency plans. The have-nots, like me, collected bargain goods and sold them on the sidewalks of Dong Khanh Street in downtown Cho Lon in order to earn a few *dongs* (Vietnamese currency) to survive. Every morning my brothers and I went to the wholesale market or called people who might have something to sell, anything from furniture to gold bars. I also taught English to supplement my income.

Six months passed. An order came that all low-ranking soldiers and non-commissioned officers of the former regime must report to the local precinct to pay a "blood debt" for the "crimes" they had committed and to teach them the "value of labor" in the new social order. I reported to the local precinct with hundreds of others. We were taken to a site near Cu Chi district not far from the famous Cu Chi Tunnels.

The job was to dig an irrigation canal. There were hundreds of similar projects taking place at that time in the vicinity of the former Viet Cong sanctuary base camp.

The canal was approximately three miles long, 60 feet wide, and 15 feet deep when it was all finished. We dug with shovels, spades, or any tool available, and used buckets to move mountains of dirt. The work was grueling, and the hours long — we worked from six in the morning into the night. Each day we had to meet the work quota or we would lose the privilege of going home on the weekend. Each Saturday evening we had to go home and pack our own food for the coming week. Interestingly enough, there were few complaints about the lousy conditions. Unlike the former ARVN officers, we could at least go home to see our families.

After three months of intense labor, I returned home because of my "satisfactory performance." When the canal was finally put to use, it flooded the adjacent farmland and damaged many houses nearby. Eventually they had to close the canal. All of the thousands of man-hours, wasted. Nevertheless, the government had achieved their main objective—punishing anyone who had been part of the former regime.

During the war, young men tried to avoid getting involved in dating and marriage due to the uncertainty of life. Women refrained from getting married out of fear of becoming widows. Now that peace had come to Vietnam, people were eager to catch up on what they had missed. The city came alive with a wedding boom. My church was no exception. There were usually one or two weddings each week.

One week near the end of the war, I met Pastor Lin at Luong Nhu Hoc Church. Pastor Lin was a missionary with Christian Missionary Alliance serving in Phnom Penh, the capital of Cambodia. He had escaped Cambodia by bus before the Khmer Rouge troops entered the capital city. He stayed at the church for a few days, waiting for a flight to return to Hong Kong. One evening, after sharing with me the story of his horrifying escape from Cambodia and of his missionary work there, he suddenly asked me a question.

"Tinh, do you have a girl friend?" he asked.

"Not yet."

"Why?"

"Well, I just don't want to get involved in emotional things while I'm still in the service," I replied.

"Have you noticed Mo Tran, the girl who played the piano at the church?"

"Sure, I know her well. She is very nice, but I never thought about dating her."

"Tinh, I have a strong feeling that she is the one for you," he nodded with a smile.

"How do you know?" I asked.

"You will find out yourself. Pray about it."

His suggestion caught me by surprise. He was only in town for a couple of days. How could he possibly know enough about me and Mo Tran to say we would be an excellent match? The most important thing in my life at that point was finding a way out of the country. Dating and marriage were well off my radar. I didn't want to break anyone's heart when I suddenly vanished.

Mo Tran (Joyce) was unique out of all the female friends in my social circle. Her father was paralyzed in a job-related accident when she was ten years old. Two years later her mother died of pneumonia, leaving a disabled husband to take care of three children. After graduating from high school, Joyce took a job as an elementary school teacher to support the family. She also taught piano lessons to supplement her family's needs. What caught my attention was the way she smiled — it was beautiful, genuine, and showed her authentic care for others. Joyce loved children and was kind to the elderly.

Deciding to follow Pastor Lin's advice, I asked her out for a drink one afternoon. We sat at an outdoor café next to the main market place. The place was humid and hot, but quiet. We ordered drinks and snacks and spent the next two hours talking about our relationship and our future. Our conversation went extremely well, except our drinks and snacks never came. I reordered several times. Either they ignored us, or possibly some invisible power kept them away while we were discussing the most urgent issue of our lives. At the end, we walked away without spending a penny. It was the cheapest date I ever had. Since we knew each other so well, we decided to ask both of our parents' permission to date and, eventually, to get married.

Monday, March 22, 1976, on a hot, sunny afternoon, 300 guests packed the small church for our wedding ceremony. It was standing room only. The air was stagnant and humid despite all the ceiling fans running at full speed. The wedding was simple, yet ceremonious. The reception menu was pound cake and iced tea, the only treat we could afford for the guests. After paying for all the expenses, we had no more money left for a honeymoon.

We rented a small apartment from a longtime friend Mrs. Ho, near Hoa Binh market, and planned to start a family. Life was tough and getting tougher. Inflation went sky high. The government abolished the "puppet" money in exchange for a new currency with a ratio of 500 to 1 *dong* (piaster). Thus, people had less cash to spend. The unemployment rate was more than seventy percent. More than two million former government officials, veterans, and their immediate dependents were denied job opportunities in the new regime.

May 8, 1976, a little over a year after the fall of Saigon, the new regime began to expel all foreign reporters, UN and Red Cross representatives from Saigon. A month later they officially announced the establishment of a "People's Tribunal" to punish anyone who had any connection with the former regime, and every businessman who had "sucked the blood" of the working class. I had anticipated all along that this revenge would come.

On July 2, 1976, upon the establishment of the unified communist Socialist Republic of Vietnam, the city of Saigon was renamed Ho Chi Minh City in honor of the late Communist leader Ho Chi Minh. With this reunification, the NLF was officially dissolved. Thus, the North Vietnamese Central Government had full control over the affairs of South Vietnam.

In early March 1977, the new government launched the "Purge and Property Inventory" campaign. Within days, hundreds of *bo doi* (government cadres) swarmed the marketplaces, business districts and homes of Chinese merchants in the city. They moved into their houses and conducted inventories of goods and merchandise, confiscated gold pieces, diamonds, jewelry, cash and anything else of value. The owners had to report their assets, everything from houses to kitchen appliances. If the search of the house revealed any discrepancy from what they originally reported, the owner would be subject to a prison term, or the whole family could be expelled from their house to the "new economic zone." Suddenly the whole city was in chaos and fear. Overnight, possession of any valuable item became a curse.

People were so frightened they destroyed whatever commodities or materials they deemed to be a risk to their lives. My next door neighbor, who was in the textile dye business, dumped hundreds of kilograms of color dye into the sewage drain behind his backyard. It turned a small, smelly creek nearby into a colorful waterway. Even the local public security could not figure out where the colorful water came from. Yet no one took time to investigate it. A few people scavenged a garbage dump near my house. They turned up jewelry, diamonds and many valuable items. This sparked a scavenging frenzy by people from a nearby housing slum.

Every day there were rumors flying around town. No one knew what was true or whether the government just wanted to spread false information to scare people. One day, a friend who worked in the precinct rushed to my house to inform my father our house was on the search order and that within hours the cadres would arrive. My mom was frantic, trying to get rid of any items that might cause trouble. In a panic, she dumped a whole box of laundry detergent into the sink drain and then tried to flush it out, filling the sink with bubbles. It took us two days to get the sink working again. In the end, this was a false alarm. The address on the search order was an error.

Soon there were plainclothes agents keeping surveillance on every street corner. Anyone who walked outside could be subjected to a search. Even people going grocery shopping had to conceal meat and any valuable commodities for fear of being questioned by the local public security. Those who were rich and famous, especially many Chinese ethnics in Cho Lon, became homeless and penniless overnight. They wandered on the streets. Many had to rely on relatives and friends for shelter and food.

My wealthy neighbor, Mr. Lam, owned a thread factory down the street and lived in a three-story building. It was the most luxurious house in my neighborhood. One morning, the *bo doi* came to his house with a search warrant. That evening, under the cover of darkness he smuggled out a bag of gold leaves, a total of 72 pieces (each piece weighed 1.2 troy ounces). He came to see my father and asked him to store the precious items for him.

"Mr. Luc, I beg you to store this bag of gold for me," he insisted. "I will reward you after the search is over."

"Where am I supposed to hide them?" my father asked.

"Wherever you think will work. If they find out I have that many gold leaves, I will be in bigger trouble. Please help me!" he insisted.

My father was a person who would not walk away from a friend in need. So he reluctantly agreed, even though he knew it would be a risk to his family. When I got home that evening, my father handed me the bag of gold. It was up to me to figure out how to deal with it.

That night I placed the bag of gold under my pillow and contemplated my next move. The next morning, I started taking apart the metal assembly of some idle textile machines. I hid all the gold leaves inside the assembly then resealed it with greasy lubricant. I assured my father that no one would ever discover it, even if the *bo doi* came in with a metal detector.

A few days later my cousin Tim Le came to see me. He was frantically panicking, as if demon possessed. Like many Chinese merchants, Tim worked all of his life to build his fortune in the cooking oil business. Now it all ended up in the hands of the new regime. He handed me a paper bag and wanted me to store it for him. He quickly turned around and walked out of my house before I could even ask another question.

Tim was a stingy merchant. He hoarded every single penny for himself. Now his fortune turned out to be his curse. I went to the back room and opened the bag he left behind. There, spread before me, were more than 50 pieces of gold leaves and 5,000 U.S. dollars in 100-dollar bills. Suddenly I found in my possession more gold than I could handle. How was I supposed to hide all of this precious metal? One thing for certain was that I could not keep it in my house. Instead, I decided to put the bag of gold in a place that would not be suspected by anyone — outside the house.

There was a cavity above the top of the entry door to my house. It was at least eight feet above the ground and not easily seen from the outside. The next morning, I got a bucket of water and a wooden ladder and climbed up to the cavity, pretending to be window washing. I dropped the bag of precious items into the cavity and covered it with a piece of wood. It worked out perfectly. No one realized that above them was a treasure of gold when they walked through the front door of my house.

One afternoon I went to Luong Nhu Hoc Church. Hoa Yen, a church friend of mine, met me at the gate. He took me inside and then pulled out from his pocket a stack of U.S. dollar bills, all in hundreds. He said it was his savings for a planned boat trip to leave the country and asked me to store it for him. I kept trying to tell him that I had no places to hide any valuable items. He insisted that his family had been expelled from his house. I had to help him out.

I knew I could no longer bring anything valuable home. So I divided the cash into two stacks, coiled them up tightly, inserted them into the handle bars of my junky, old bicycle and concealed them with two black covers. Every day I rode this "dollar" bike around town with a chain and lock to make sure no one could walk away with it.

Everyone in the city was gripped by the fear. They wondered who would become the next victim of the *bo doi*. Fortunately my father's small textile factory, which had been closed down for more than a year, would probably not be a target of search by the government any time soon.

Meanwhile, a new class of the "suddenly rich" emerged from the ashes of capitalism. They were former North Vietnamese Army soldiers who became local officials. They once fought in the jungle and most of them had never seen a light bulb or a motorcycle in their lives. Now they were in charge of the governing positions in the South. It did not take long for these hillbillies to realize that their newfound positions were the way to a new life of comfort and enjoyment. They bought lofty houses, automobiles, jewelry and television sets with the money they confiscated from the searches. They collaborated with the local gangsters and schemed to sell the government's properties. Soon those high-ranking government officials owned every automobile on the street. Fancy restaurants and bars were frequent gathering places of the new rich and their friends who owned all the wealth in town.

Was it possible to take a flight out of the country? Some of my friends could buy fake passports to take a flight out to India and then to countries in Europe and beyond. They had to have the help of comrades in the Ministry of Foreign Affairs in downtown Ho Chi Minh City. After three short years in power, the ideology underlying the liberation of the South from American imperialism had been thrown out the window. In its place was rampant corruption in all levels of government. It was far worse than the former regime that they had overthrown not so long ago.

The campaign of Purge and Property Inventory ended nine months later. It left behind a shattered economy and many people unemployed and homeless. Inflation skyrocketed. Many lost their desire to stay and began planning to flee the country by any means, even giving up everything they had accumulated for many generations. Some of my friends suddenly vanished and later it was confirmed they had escaped by taking fishing boats out of the country. A few reportedly arrived in Malaysia and the Hong Kong refugee camps. Others were never heard from again. Some others even took a risky trip by foot through Cambodia to Thailand. Obviously, making these trips required large sums of cash or gold that only the rich could afford. With the mediocre income I made, it was unlikely I could afford the trip any time soon.

As the situation began to calm down, I decided to return all the valuable items that my friends had entrusted my family to store for them during the height of the search.

My wealthy neighbor, Mr. Lam, came over one evening. He was grateful for my help and decided to lend 30 pieces of gold leaves to my family. He told me to use it to find a way to flee the country.

"Tinh, there is no hope to stay here anymore." He patted my shoulder. "Take a risk so that you and your children will have a better future in another country."

I thanked him for his generosity and promised to repay him once we resettled.

I was so excited now that I had the capital on hand. However, finding passage to get out was a different story. Of all the options relying on elaborate and clandestine means, escaping by boat was the most feasible with the least cost. The payment usually ranged from 8 to 12 gold leaves per person since the Vietnamese currency *dong* had no value in this business.

Meanwhile, Joyce became pregnant with our first child. The whole family, especially my mother, was overjoyed by the news. However, her pregnancy made finding a passage more complicated and difficult. Most underground boat organizers would not take a pregnant woman or family with a baby for fear of exposing their plot to the coast guard patrolling the coastline. And at that time, the public health department of the city was promoting family planning, particularly abortion. It was widely available and the procedure and hospital stay was free. It was unthinkable that the health department could be more eager to get rid of the unborn than to feed the hungry. Obviously Joyce and I had no intention of having an abortion. The unborn is a created, living human being inside a mother's womb, no matter how one looks at it. For us, terminating a pregnancy for the sake of the convenience of seeking passage to leave the country was not only selfish and immoral, but it would be an act of murder.

My mother insisted Joyce and I must go together, as soon as we could find a passage, because of my background with the U.S. military. As dangerous as it might be to escape while Joyce was pregnant, bringing a newborn baby on a journey across the South China Sea in a tiny boat deemed extremely dangerous. Time was not on our side anymore.

I now actively searched every lead through friends and relatives. I had been extremely cautious because the arrangement was considered illegal. Quite often the government set up traps to bait innocents for gold and to arrest those who were involved. The first contact I made was with a friend who claimed to own a fishing boat in Phan Thiet in central Vietnam. He said the boat was ready to depart as soon as the weather permitted. Soon after I gave the deposit of three pieces of gold leaves, he called off the trip. He claimed his boat was confiscated by the local authorities. He refused to return the deposit because he had used it for the cost of the boat.

Two months later, a friend of mine told me he had made a deposit for a boat trip in Vung Tau, southeast of Ho Chi Minh City. I met the boat owner and personally went to see the actual fishing boat myself. I made the deposit and waited for the departing day. Three months went by without any information. When I demanded the return of my deposit, he refused. We had no way to know whether he intended to deceive us or not. Both my friend and I lost yet another deposit. Suing him was impossible because we were already operating outside the law. It would land both of us in jail.

I was so frustrated with the loss. It seemed there wasn't a boat owner out there whom I could trust. I came home one evening and my landlady Mrs. Ho said she had some good news. One of her nephews owned a boat and was ready to leave within days. However, it had only one opening available and the deadline was the next day. This certainly was more reliable, because we had known Mrs. Ho for many years. Now I had a dilemma. If I decided to go by myself, how could I leave Joyce behind?

That night Joyce and I lay in bed, starring at the blank white ceiling, unable to sleep. We wrested with the decision we should make.

On one hand, it could be the only chance for me to leave the country for good. On the other, we had been married a little more than two years and we loved each other dearly. Joyce was five months pregnant. Separation was unthinkable, let alone taking a trip so risky that no one could guarantee whether we might ever see each other again. We struggled all night. We embraced and wept together. Finally, we knelt beside the bed and prayed. We vowed to be together, regardless of whether we stayed or left. We submitted to God's will, asking Him to open the door for us to leave the country together.

On June 16, 1978, our daughter Irene was born. She was healthy and adorable. I have never seen any girl as beautiful. My parents rejoiced for their first grandchild and invited relatives and friends to my house for her first month's celebration which was a Chinese tradition.

During that time, Vietnam and the Soviet Union signed the Treaty of Friendship and Cooperation. However, China considered it a military alliance and a threat to their security. Military incidents increased dramatically along the Sino-Vietnamese border. In December 1978, Vietnam invaded Cambodia. Within days, it ousted the pro-Beijing Khmer Rouge regime. In February 1979, China responded by invading the bordering provinces of Vietnam.

In order to minimize the Chinese influence in Vietnam, especially in the south where more than one million Chinese ethnics lived in Cho Lon, the Ha Noi central government secretly launched an "ethnic cleansing campaign" in the form of driving all Chinese out to sea, regardless if they lived or died. They instructed that every city along the 1000-mile-long coastline in the south must collect gold leaves, and then let all the Chinese leave the country by boat.

Although the Hanoi government meant it for evil, the Chinese ethnics saw this as a golden opportunity to leave the country and seek better lives in other parts of the world. There were also many South Vietnamese intellectuals, including doctors, professors, engineers and lawyers, who saw no hope for their future in the new regime. They, too, decided to leave their motherland despite the risk. Suddenly the whole city was talking about a massive exodus. Buying and selling boats became the hottest business in town. At every seaport along the southern coast, new boat builders could not keep up with the demands. Everyone tried to get out as soon as possible before the government changed its mind. Of course, the biggest winners were the local public security officers who were in charge of the exodus. U.S. dollars and gold leaves flew into their coffers faster than they could count them.

Despite the fact that the venture was under the auspices of the local government officials and most of the boats were better prepared for the trip than those that had gone before, the risk was still extremely high. In March 1978, a well-modified cargo ship owned by several wealthy Chinese merchants was getting ready to set sail from Cat Lai Port on Dong Nai River near Ho Chi Minh City. As they completed the boarding, the boat suddenly broke loose from the pier and flipped over, drowning everyone on board. The owners stood at the pier, watching helplessly as the tragedy unfolded. Their families were among the dead. The next day the local authorities recovered more than 700 bodies. It was just one of many tragedies that happened so often during this period of exodus. Two of my cousins and a family of five, who were very close to me, set sail from a seaport not far from Ho Chi Minh City, and I never heard from them again.

Despite the outcry by international communities, the Hanoi government saw this as a win-win situation. They thought nothing could be better than collecting gold leaves from Chinese ethnics, and all the while ridding themselves of Chinese influence within their borders.

CHAPTER 2

Boat PK3399

Ma Quang was an honest businessman. For decades, his father owned a rice depot near my house. One day he approached me saying he had a fishing boat in Vung Tau, a seaport southeast of Ho Chi Minh City. He asked me to come and see for myself, and maybe I would be interested in joining him in this adventure. By now I was extremely cautious and decided to investigate thoroughly before I made a move.

The boat with the registration number PK3399 was in dry dock for modifications. It was a well-constructed wooden fishing boat in comparison with other boats I had seen. It was 90 feet long and 30 feet wide with a 200hp engine. In order to convert it into a boat suitable to carry at least 200 passengers, they added several wooden planks along the length in the lower interior deck, as well as on the upper deck for passenger seating. They had also installed two galvanized air vents for circulation in the lower deck and a canvas roof on the top deck with wood beam supports for shelter from the harsh elements at sea. The wheel house and cabin compartment had been painted green. At the stern they added a small kitchen and an outhouse with a canvas curtain. Later on, they installed a piece of steel bracket to strengthen the bow of the boat.

I also met Ma Quang's local partner, Mr. Au Thanh, who was in charge of getting boarding permits from the local public security chief. If things went as anticipated and according to what they said, PK3399 would set sail within a month. They only needed the local public security chief's approval and enough passengers to fill the boat. I checked some references. It seemed they were dependable business-men who intended to leave the country on the boat with their own families.

I decided to put in my deposit. I also asked a few more friends to join me. Ma Quang also agreed to hire my brother Tri (Marvin) as the manager of the boat. He waived his fee, which was an enormous help for my family. However, after two months had gone by, we still had not received approval from the security chief. To my surprise, I discovered Au Thanh had tricked Ma Quang into signing over the ownership of the boat to him.

Not only that, Au Thanh apparently had no desire to see the boat sail. He partied and got drunk day and night. He hired prostitutes and even married his mistress with the approval of his wife. He not only squandered most of the gold deposits other people had given to Ma Quang, but also threatened to sell the boat and pocket the profit if we kept bothering him.

This unexpected twist dragged on for more than six months. We tried everything to convince Au Thanh to give up the title of the boat and allow us to set sail, but he just ignored our plea. Meanwhile, those who had given deposits to Ma Quang demanded the return of their deposit. A few even threatened to kill him. In desperation, he sold everything he had down to the furniture in his house. Nevertheless, he still could not repay what he owed.

With all our savings invested in this venture, I was stuck with this raw deal — do or die. It seemed my hope of a journey to freedom had gone down the drain once again, along with the gold leaves I had bor-rowed and promised to repay. These friends who I had asked to join me on the trip also blamed me for their loss. They threatened to ruin my family if Ma Quang refused to return their payments. I begged them to give me more time and promised to repay them once the boat set sail.

One morning I had breakfast in a cafe with Ma Quang and some of his friends who also suffered the same fate as I did. The conversation was depressing because we had exhausted all options. Then I noticed a man at the next table looking at me. Later he came over to join us for coffee.

"Are you Mr. Luc Dang's son?" he asked me.

"Yes," I replied.

"My name is Tran Lam. You may not remember me, but your father was my master for many years when I first learned the trade of the textile business. He is a good man. I was always grateful for his help when I first came to him."

I was surprised. Someone still remembered my father after all these years. Then he told me he was building a brand new jumbo-sized passenger boat with the capacity of holding more than 500 passengers. He and his partner, Sa Day, were getting ready to set sail once the boat could be furnished with an engine and water pumps, and with the help of the Bien Hoa public security chief Sau Thanh, a well-known figure in the exodus business in Dong Nai province.

I told Tran Lam of the dilemma we were facing and that we needed his help. He offered to take my case before Sau Thanh. I promised if things turned in our favor, I would repay him by taking the boat to Dong Nai Province under his arrangements.

Two days later he came to me with the good news that Sau Thanh agreed to intervene. However, the only problem was Au Thanh was a resident of another province and he and his boat were outside Dong Nai's jurisdiction. He promised that if we could somehow bring Au Thanh to his territory then he would arrest him and bring him to justice.

We were excited by the news. It certainly was a God-send. Now we had a chance to turn things around.

At a gathering of "The Gang of PK3399" (those who had invested their savings in this boat trip), I came up with a plan that shocked everyone. I explained to them that we must trick Au Thanh to come to see Ma Quang, then make a move to arrest him. The plot sounded convincing, but everyone had doubts from the beginning whether it would work. Besides, it could have an unintended consequence if it failed. Au Thanh could carry out his threat of selling the boat, then pocketing the proceeds.

"Look," I was getting impatient. "All we want is to make Au Thanh hand over the ownership of the boat without resorting to violence. Obviously this plan has some risks. Nevertheless, it is much better than not acting and letting Au Thanh squander everything we had. Unless we act now, with the help of Sau Thanh, I do not see any other way. Besides, all I need is few people to carry out the plot."

Finally, everyone had no choice but to agree with my plan.

I chose a few "actors" to take part in the plot. Obviously, Ma Quang had to play a key role in the whole scheme. He needed to throw a party at his house and invite Au Thanh to attend. He also needed to recruit his friend Cang, the local precinct security chief, for help. Cang somehow sympathized with Ma Quang and his plight and was more than happy to detain Au Thanh momentarily.

Long Phu, who had invested all of his savings in this trip, wanted to be part of it because he had the highest stakes in the boat. He told me that he would lose everything if the trip turned out to be a failure. Phat and his wife had been expelled from their home by the government during the "Search and Inventory Campaign." Angered by this delay, Phat voluntarily joined in because he wanted the excitement of putting Au Thanh in jail. I also convinced Ma Quang's relatives and neighbors to attend, so the party looked more like a family celebration. Of course, I had to be there to oversee the entire operation.

The evening came and everything went as planned. As all the guests gathered at Ma Quang's house, Au Thanh arrived on time as an honored guest. We toasted rice wine and enjoyed roasted duck and barbecued pork, and we had a good time. It went well into the night and passed curfew hours. The curfew law required everyone to return to his own residence before nine o'clock in the evening. Violators were subject to fines or even prison terms. Suddenly, the precinct security chief Cang and his men knocked on the door. They pretended to be conducting a routine search and found the gathering illegal and ordered everyone involved detained. He escorted everyone back to the police station. Once Au Thanh was locked up in the cell, the rest of us were allowed to go home.

Early the next morning, I notified the office of Dong Nai Provincial Public Security Bureau that Au Thanh was behind bars. Sau Thanh immediately sent his men to the precinct's lockup to extradite Au Thanh back to Dong Nai prison.

For three days, Au Thanh sat in the dark prison cell, puzzled and scared, unable to eat or drink. He did not have the slightest idea why he was in prison. One morning he was led into an interrogation room full of people. Waiting for him there was Ma Quang, Long Phu and the rest of the Gang of PK3399. Au Thanh dropped to his knees, weeping and begging for mercy. Ma Quang demanded that he hand over the ownership of the boat, unconditionally. Au Thanh agreed and promised to give up the title. Everyone enjoyed the drama playing out in the room and felt that justice had finally been served.

Soon after that he was let out of prison. A week later, when we asked him to sign the transfer document, he demanded that we include his brother and his family of four to travel with us, free of charge, before he would sign over the ownership. We tentatively agreed with him in order to keep the process moving. Within a month, Au Thanh boarded another boat to flee the country for fear we might lock him up again.

Meanwhile, Ma Quang felt that his mismanagement of the boat had caused more pain for everyone involved and had depleted all the gold deposits which others entrusted to him. He willingly gave up his ownership. The Gang of PK3399 designated Long Phu and mysef as the new representatives. Sau Thanh also designated Sa Day, Tran Lam's partner, as the main contact to manage the process for getting the boat permit to leave the country.

With the title in hand, we took the boat from a pier near Vung Tau to Pier 73 north of Ba Ria, within the territory of Dong Nai Province as we had promised the provincial police chief. However, as the boat cruised along the narrow inlet toward the new location, the engine stalled. It drifted for hours before we could find someone willing to tow it to the dock. We decided to rebuild the boat engine before setting sail again.

By early May 1979, preparation of the boat went into high gear. The final repairs had been completed and we bought one large compass and one small, handheld military compass for back up. We stocked up on diesel fuel and water containers. My brother Marvin took charge of the day-to-day operation of the boat. My other, mechanically-gifted brother Toan (Tony) also decided to join us because we were in need of a dependable mechanic. His primary job was to rebuild the only boat engine onboard. In all, seven members of my family took part in the boat trip: Marvin, Tony, my two younger brothers Jason and Andrew, my wife Joyce, our eleven month-old daughter Irene, and myself. My father, initially, rejected the idea of having so many members of his family traveling in the same boat, a stake too high for him to accept. Nevertheless it was the only opportunity we could afford, given our limited resources.

Things went so well that I expected we would set sail within a week. Then something happened that almost derailed the whole journey. One evening in late May, I was staying at Long Phu's house while Phat was there to help me complete the final roster. We needed to submit a list the next day to the Dong Nai Public Security for approval. We worked past curfew hours, assuming it was not a big deal to stay overnight once in a while. At midnight, the local precinct conducted a routine search in the neighborhood and discovered both Phat and I staying there illegally. They ordered us to follow them to the station. At that moment, Phat pretended to suffer a seizure. He convulsed on the floor, not able to walk. The officer allowed him to stay in the house for the night with the promise that Long Phu would turn him in to the station the next morning.

I stayed in a jail cell in the 13th precinct office overnight. I assumed that it was my first offense and Joyce would have no problem bailing me out the next morning. But the next morning Phat did not show up. By ten o'clock, Bay, the precinct sergeant, promptly sent his men to Long Phu's house. To his dismay Long Phu and Phat had both fled. Only his sister-in law, Yen, and her two children stayed in the house. Bay was furious and demanded that I must disclose where Phat was hiding. I told him that I had no idea where Phat lived. He was not convinced.

"You must tell me the truth or I'll lock you up for good," he screamed at me as he pounded on the table.

"Sir, I don't even know where he lives," I answered.

"Listen." He stood up, leaned over his desk and pressed his finger on my forehead. "I want to know what you guys were doing in the house in the middle of the night!"

"I just was visiting the owner of the house and did not realize I stayed past the curfew hours. I'm sorry about that," I stated.

"You are lying!" He raged and screamed. "We had that house under surveillance for the last couple of days. I saw people coming and going all day long. There must be something going on in the house. You tell me everything or I'll lock you up for good."

I sensed something serious was going to happen. If Phat did not turn himself in soon, I would be in more trouble than I could think of. Organizing a boat trip to leave the country was an open secret in town, paying a fine would get me off the hook. If I were suspected of counter-revolutionary or conspiratorial activities, then I could be subjected to torture and brutal interrogation. I decided to tell him everything.

"Sir, Long Phu, the house owner, has a boat. He is preparing to leave the country, so I came to join him. As you know, the central government allows all Chinese ethnics to leave the country by boat," I finally confessed.

"I will still lock you up until I know the truth." He was still not convinced.

At that moment, Joyce came in with the proper document to bail me out. She was shocked to learn that I would probably be sent to the Third District Headquarters for further interrogation.

I was taken back to the dark, damp, windowless jail cell. All morning I thought about Joyce and Irene. What if I were sent to the district headquarters? What was my family supposed to do? If the boat could set sail on schedule, then I would rather have them go without me, given I had invested so much already on this journey. While I tried to figure out what to do next, I prayed that somehow God would get me out of jail and allow me to join them soon.

Since I was returned to the jail cell, Joyce realized something had gone wrong. She rushed to see her brother Dai Vay at his office. He was a manager of a government-owned plastic products company. As they contemplated what to do next, one of Dai Vay's customers named Hoa, happened to walk in and heard of my arrest. He offered to come to the rescue. It turned out Hoa was a former North Vietnamese Army officer, and the police chief of the 13th Precinct was his subordinate during the war. He assured Joyce that he would do everything to secure my release.

That afternoon the guard took me to the precinct chief's office. Standing there was a man in his thirties, dressed in a loose blue shirt.

"I'm Hoa," he introduced himself to me. "Your brother-in-law, Dai Vay, is my good friend. He told me that you were in trouble, so I came to get you out. Don't worry, you will be OK. It may take a couple more days to work out the arrangements."

I thanked him for his help. He would not tell me any more details, and only said he would be back to the next day to see me.

That evening they allowed me to stay in the lobby of the precinct office instead of the dark, windowless cell. With the front gate wide open I could have walked out without anyone noticing. However, I would rather not jeopardize the negotiation that was still in progress. I lay on a broken wooden bench, the only piece of furniture in the lobby. I slept unusually well through the night as if nothing had happened. I was calm and at peace.

The next morning I went to the bathroom to clean up. While I was there, I suddenly realized there was a copy of the boat title in my wallet that specified I was one of the primary representatives of PK3399. I quickly tore it into pieces and flushed it into the toilet. As I was returning to the lobby, sergeant Bay ordered me into his office.

"You must tell me who you are. You're not telling the truth." His voice was somewhat calm and friendly.

"Sir, I've already told you everything yesterday," I said.

"Take everything out from your pockets, now!" he demanded, his tone changed.

I did as he instructed, and placed everything on the table before him, including my wallet. He carefully examined each piece of paper without saying a word. After a while, he returned them to me and told me to stay in the lobby and wait for his decision. I was glad that I had destroyed the boat title contract before I was called into his office, otherwise the outcome could have been different.

Hoa arrived at the precinct chief's office that afternoon for the final arrangements. Then he came over to see me. He said he had worked out a deal to release me. He had brought in the "ransom money" and I would be released in a couple of hours. I expressed my gratitude for his help. Soon Bay called me into his office. He returned my ID and told me to go home. I walked down the street. My brother Tony was waiting for me at a corner cafe with his motorcycle to take me home.

Joyce greeted me as I arrived at her father's house. Irene was there with her. She then told me that the ransom money, a total of five pieces of gold, was paid for from the coffers of the boat.

That evening Hoa came to see me. He wanted to make sure I was home safe. He also told me something about how serious my arrest was. While I was locked up in the precinct, the Ho Chi Minh City Intelligence Bureau had confirmed two Chinese spies had infiltrated into Cho Lon for subversive activities. The whole city was on alert. A manhunt was on for the spies. Initially, the precinct commander thought I was one of the spies and was about to send me to the city headquarters for interrogation. Without Hoa's intervention, the outcome would have been much worse.

The next morning I went to see Sa Day. He told me he had put everything on hold, pending my release. He no longer trusted Long Phu and Phat because they had abandoned me when I was arrested and insisted that I would be the only one making decisions about the boat. He handed me a roster of 351 people who would be part of the journey.

"Three-hundred-fifty-one passengers jammed in a tiny boat. Are you crazy?" I was getting angry. "How can I pack that many passengers in such a tiny boat? Do you understand we are human beings, not sardines? It is impossible to fit everyone in."

"Tinh, calm down!" Sa Day tried to explain. "It was the decision made by the Dong Nai Public Security Office. I have no other choice. They are the ones that make the final call. They demanded a certain amount of gold before they let you go."

I was outraged. I knew something like this might happen from the beginning, but not to this extent. I should have known better by now. The intention of the rogue government was to kick every Chinese out to the high seas. They did not care whether we survived or not, so long as they had collected enough gold from us before we left. Time was running out and there was no need to argue.

I spent the next couple of days finalizing every detail for Sa Day. Then I waited for the day of departure.

– CHAPTER 3 –

The Journey at Sea

Monday morning, June 4, 1979, was the first day of Vacation Bible School (VBS) for my church. It was a fun gathering of more than 200 children from the neighborhood. Initially the local public security denied permission for such gatherings citing that the atheist regime's long-held policy prohibited churches from sharing Christianity with children of non-Christian families. The church explained that these were children of church members who were gathering to study the Bible. Finally, the local authority allowed the program to proceed.

Joyce was playing the piano for the singers while I took care of Irene. By ten o'clock, two plainclothes public security officers arrived from the 5th District Headquarters and demanded to see the pastor of the church. They wore white shirts and the shorter officer also donned a pair of sunglasses. I invited both of them into the church office and we sat down. They were polite, yet suspicious. They wanted to see for themselves what the gathering was, and asked a wide range of questions regarding the church.

As the conversation was about to end, one of the officers said, "Recently, there have been a lot of Chinese ethnics leaving the country. What is the position of the church on this issue?"

We did not expect they would ask this question. The pastor replied, "Sir, this is a personal choice. The church neither encourages nor discourages anyone from making their own decision."

While I was in the meeting, Sa Day walked into the church. He wanted to talk to me. I excused myself from the meeting and took Sa Day outside. He told me the boat would be ready to depart that evening. My family and I were to arrive at the pier no later than five in the afternoon.

I immediately took Joyce and Irene home. After packing my luggage, I went to my father's house to say goodbye. We picked up Jason and Andrew (Marvin and Tony had stayed with the boat for the last three weeks), and hurried to the bus station for the two-hour bus ride to Pier 73 near Ba Ria. As we arrived, there was a sizeable crowd already gathered in a tin-roof hangar near the pier. However, there were no public security representatives on site. The departure was postponed until the next day. We settled down in a corner of the hangar for the night.

The next morning, June 5, the pier was full of people. Everyone was excited that the big day had finally arrived. However, I sensed there was also a feeling of uneasiness among the crowd. As they watched the parade of boats at the pier, PK3399 was rickety and small in comparison to others. They hesitated and wondered whether this boat could safely deliver them to the other shore.

By ten o'clock in the morning, as I was loading the food supplies, Long Phu and Phat came to tell me that Au Thanh's brother and his family of four had arrived at the pier demanding to get on board. Since their names were not supposed to be on the boarding roster, I told them not to make contact with him. I did not want to cause any disturbance at the pier before departure. The public security representatives would handle them afterwards.

My father came to the pier to see us off. He was still uneasy about the whole situation. With seven of his children and his only grandchild leaving, he was taking an enormous risk. Nevertheless, he understood it was the only hope for the future of his family. I told him to pray for us every day and I would send a telegram once we reached our destination.

Early in the afternoon, the representatives from the provincial public security office arrived and made a final inspection of the boat and we began the boarding process.

We assigned the younger people to the lower deck and the elderly stayed on the upper level. The mothers with small babies were allowed to stay in the small cabin behind the wheel room. As we were completing the boarding process, suddenly, the boat started tilting to one side. It was overloaded! Skipper Xe, an experienced fisherman who we hired to pilot the boat, ordered the crew to throw out food supplies and unnecessary equipment. I realized that no matter how skillful a skipper was, keeping this tiny fishing boat afloat with 351 people on board would be quite a challenge. However, it was too late to terminate the trip. Meanwhile, there was a disturbance at the dock. Au Thanh's brother and his family were not allowed to board because their names were not on the boarding roster. They protested, and the police had to fire warning shots to disperse the crowd.

At five o'clock, everything was ready. The boat departed from Pier 73 under the escort of a provincial navy patrol boat. I stood next to the wheel house, watching it steadily and slowly navigate through the narrow inlets of Dong Nai River as we headed toward the open sea. This was the moment I had been waiting for. I was excited, yet nervous. Looking at everyone's faces around me, I was not the only one.

We held on to our meager possessions and crowded into this rickety and over-packed boat. We were embarking on a journey with an unknown destination, fleeing the country we once loved, leaving behind our childhood homes. We were taking a gamble with our lives by sailing into the roaring sea searching for freedom and opportunity, with no regrets and no desire to return. We only hoped the risk we took would eventually pay off and the new lives we found on foreign shores would be better than the lives we had reluctantly left behind.

As the boat chugged into the beautiful sunset, no one realized that the humble and rickety boat was the last one to leave Pier 73. Within a week, the Central Government in Hanoi issued an emergency decree to halt all boat exodus operations nationwide. Apparently, Ha Noi had given in under the international pressure to stop this inhumane activity. They also confiscated all the boats. Boat owners were arrested and indicted for subversive activities. Within a month, Tran Lam and Sa Day were both arrested and later sentenced to six months in prison. Their jumbo-sized fancy boat named DN747, which was supposed to set sail within days, was also confiscated. Even Sau Thanh, the powerful Dong Nai Public Security Chief, was not immune. I was later told he was convicted of corruption charges and sentenced to five years in prison. The timing of our boat's departure was obviously beyond our control. Many people believe we were the lucky few.

One year later, after he was released from prison, Sa Day came to see my father. He said to my father, in his own words, "Tinh is the luckiest guy in the whole world." For me, this was another example of God's timing and purpose in everything I do.

By dusk, we had passed the Vung Tau port. The navy patrol boat bid farewell to us and returned to its base. Now we were all by ourselves, churning forward with full speed in the dark sea. The night was peaceful except for the chug-chug of the boat engine, the pounding of white waves against the hull, and once in a while, the cry of babies on board.

It was already past midnight but I still could not sleep. I went down to the engine room to see Tony. For the next six days and nights, he stayed alone in this dark, noisy and filthy room, without much sleep, in order to keep the engine and water pump running. From time to time, he filled up buckets of water to dump over the side of the boat when the water pumps could not keep up with the rising water in the bottom hold of the boat. He told me the engine was performing well so far, in large part because of his overhaul before setting sail.

The next morning was sunny and the sea was calm. I climbed up to the poop deck (above the cabin) to look around. We were now far away from land. I looked over to the west. I saw the mountain peaks of Con Son Island emerging over the horizon. Assuming we were now sailing in international waters, I told Skipper Xe the good news. He, in turn, made an announcement that we were finally out of Vietnamese territory. Everyone was rejoicing and excited. The cook prepared a large pot of hot coffee mixed with condensed milk, for everyone on board for the celebration. The boat had limited food supplies for all passengers. Each person had to bring their own dried rations, enough for the journey.

I was on the poop deck for the rest of the morning. I searched the horizon, hoping to spot any ship or vessels passing by that could render help, or perhaps tow us to the nearest port. I had never been out on the open sea in all of my life. It was so beautiful, yet surreal.

That evening the sea was getting rough. I sent a couple of men to tighten the canvas over the upper deck to make sure it was secured. Dark clouds blackened the sky and then flashes of lightning and rumblings and peals of thunder came over the horizon. Soon heavy rain poured in. The winds whipped the seas into a frenzy. The waves surged over and pounded the bow of the boat and hurled the boat up, then smacked it down as if it was a toy. I took cover in the wheel room where Skipper Xe was battling the raging sea. He seemed calm and in control. He told me it was common to encounter thunderstorms this time of the year. He hoped the steel brace, which we had installed to strengthen the boat before our departure, would prove to be strong enough to hold the boat together, or all of us would perish.

"The only difference is the cargo, this time it is people and not fish.

Now we have over three hundred human souls on board," he said.

Xe told me to instruct everyone to hang tight. He did not want to see anyone falling overboard. However, trying to calm everyone down in the midst of the raging sea was another story. Young and old were crying and screaming in horror. Some ladies were howling, crying, that we were going to drown if we did not turn around and head back to shore. I tried to calm them down to no avail.

Suddenly a horrified passenger burst into the wheel room. He was wet, shivering, and clearly panicking. He fell to the floor and begged: "Mr. Skipper, We are dying! Oh my god! My whole family will die!"

Xe tried to calm him down, "Sir, we are too far from land to return. We should be okay. You just calm down and return to your seat."

The man was not convinced, still crying and begging. I had no choice but to escort him back to his seat.

I came to the cabin where Joyce and Irene stayed. Irene also was crying in her mother's bosom. Apparently, she was frightened by the wailing noises around her. I held her tiny hands together in an attempt to comfort her.

Two hours passed and the storm finally subsided. I went around checking for damage. Everything seemed to still be intact. The passengers on the upper deck were all soaking wet from the heavy downpour, except for the few who took cover under their rain gear.

I woke up the next morning to find the sea was calm and the sky was cloudy. The boat turned southwest, heading in the direction of Malaysia and Singapore. By ten in the morning, there was a fishing boat heading in our direction at high speed. By a flag and insignia on the bow, I identified it as a Thai fishing boat. After we had exchanged conversation, the Thai fishermen seemed friendly. I asked them for food supplies. They gave me a bucket of fish before departing from us. I took the fish to the kitchen, and the cook prepared a large pot of fish porridge for everyone on board. This was the only hot meal we had during the whole journey.

As we kept track of how far we had traveled, we anticipated that if we maintained the same speed and the same course, we would reach Malaysian waters by evening the next day. It was good news to everyone on board. Most of the passengers were packed in a tight space, like sardines in a sardine can, not able to move around for the past three days. I had no idea how much longer they could stay this way. Prolonging the journey could prove to be disastrous.

– CHAPTER 4 –

Robbed by Thai Pirates

As night fell, a fishing boat went by. I recognized it as the same boat we encountered that morning, the one that had given us a basket of fish. This time they even offered to take us to Singapore. Everyone was thrilled. Of course the Thai fishing boat was four times bigger and, no doubt, a lot safer than ours. No one would pass up such an offer. We followed their instructions that all young men, including myself, climb over to their boat. They tied a rope to our boat and towed it at high speed. We all sat in a circle on the pitch dark deck, excited that we could arrive at Singapore by morning. Suddenly, the jubilation turned into a nightmare.

First I heard a gunshot. Then several bright searchlights shone upon us. I saw the Thai fishermen standing all around, carrying pistols, sharp knives and machetes. A bulky man wearing a black headband was standing on the bridge above us. He pointed his pistol at the frightened captives. Apparently he was the leader, and the fishermen were actual, modern-day pirates. He barked at us with broken English. He ordered us to stand still and raise both hands. It happened so quickly that we could not react, but followed his order. A young pirate in his twenties, wearing a sarong and a cap, was holding a machete in one hand and a steel cooking pot in the other. He walked around, barking at every shaken captive to remove all their precious belongings and put them into the pot. I gave him my wedding ring and wrist watch, but he still took my eyeglasses (Fortunately, I was still able to see without the eyeglasses).

After they had stripped us of all our belongings, the gang leader ordered us back to our own boat. Instead of letting our boat go, they towed it at high speed in the dark of the night. I immediately went to the wheel room to find Skipper Xe. He was panicking; his hand was holding a compass. "They are towing us to Thai territory! It is not over yet."

He showed me the compass. The needle pointed in a northwest direction.

We sent two guys to the bow of our boat in an attempt to cut the rope to free us, but a Thai pirate was sitting there with a pistol. Unless we eliminated him, there was no way we could free ourselves from the pirates. I asked around to see if anyone had a weapon. Someone handed me an old kitchen knife, not sharp enough to do the job. I finally abandoned the idea of revolt, accepting the fact that we just had to sit tight and let the situation take its course.

The towing journey lasted at least three hours. Presumably, we were now inside the Gulf of Thailand. By daybreak, a different Thai trawler came alongside and docked on the starboard side of our boat. Apparently the whole operation was well-planned. I noticed that the registration numbers on the bows of both ships were covered with cardboard. The pirates ordered everyone, young and old, to climb into the trawler. The sea was rough, and the boats were crashing against each other violently, making the climb into the trawler extremely dangerous. I held Irene tightly to my chest and jumped over, then turned around to help Joyce and others get on board. Once we all lined up on the deck, the pirates strip-searched us one by one. Soon they collected a bucketful of gold bars, diamonds, and U.S. dollars. They found a bag of diamonds in the underwear of a frightened young girl who stood next to me. Anyone who resisted was subjected to strip naked.

I noticed several young girls standing behind the crowd with their heads bowed, frightened and sobbing. Their faces were smeared with black ash. Tears rolled down on their cheeks, leaving trails on their beautiful faces. First I could not figure out why they did this to themselves. Then I realized they were trying to cover their faces in hopes that the pirates would not pick on them. Everyone could not help but to laugh. Even the pirates, who strip-searched them, simply asked them to give up their possessions. It turned out that these pirates were not fearful, merciless professional Thai pirates. What we had encountered, fortunately, were Thai fishermen who set out to prey on the vulnerable and defenseless boat people for gold and precious gems. Some of them could speak Teochiew (one of the Chinese dialects commonly spoken in Thailand), and we were able to have a polite conversation with them. When we asked for drinking water, they kindly filled up all of the empty water containers on the boat. It was so ironic that an hour earlier, they had pointed their sharp knives at us. Now they helped dress the wounds for those who suffered cuts. We had lost all valuable savings, but we were grateful no one was raped, tortured or even killed during this ordeal.

Meanwhile, other pirates ransacked our boat from top to bottom, turning everything upside down, looting any valuable items they could find. After more than two hours of ransacking and looting, they allowed us to return to our boat, and then they went their own way. We tried to salvage what was left and heaped the rest into a big pile. Xe ordered everyone back to their seats. I went down to the engine room; Tony informed me the pirates did not damage the engine or the water pumps. Everything seemed to work again. It was a good sign.

After a quick clean up, we headed out to international waters and tried to get away from the pirate-infested Gulf of Thailand. By three o'clock in the afternoon another Thai fishing boat was on the horizon.

Though it was much smaller than the ones we encountered earlier, it was still more powerful than our leaky, overcrowded boat. Skipper Xe tried to maneuver to get away, but the Thai fishing boat outran us. Just when the fishing boat was about to slam into the starboard of our boat, Skipper Xe had to maneuver the boat to stop. Two pirates armed with a pistol and knife came on board and threatened to kill us all unless we handed over gold and jewelry. This time, everyone just sat still and watched. An old lady told the pirate holding a pistol that since we had been robbed twice, there would not be much left. They could take anything they wanted and let us go. However, they were not convinced. They continued to rummage through the huge pile of clothing for an hour before they took off.

We had enough of the ransacking and threatening, and found ourselves tired and hungry. We vowed to stay away from any vessel, no matter who they were. By nightfall we set sail again heading south toward Malaysia. Suddenly over the horizon I saw five large vessels. Judging from a distance by the bright lighting on their bridges, they were fishing trawlers, approaching us at high speed. Everyone was panicking and screaming.

"Xe, you need to do something!" I was panicky. Now, it was up to him to get us out of this trouble.

"We have no other choice," Marvin burst into the room, frightened. "Xe, we must run for our lives! If we get caught this time and we have nothing to offer them, they will kill all the men and rape all the women for sure!"

Xe instructed everyone to sit tight and turned off the lights on the boat. He throttled the engine to maximum speed. I watched the Thai trawlers getting closer until their bright spot lights had reached over the stern of our boat. Every time they were closing in Xe made a sharp turn, maneuvering to break away from them. The pursuit lasted more than two hours. Suddenly they turned away and stopped the pursuit.

Apparently we had entered Malaysian waters, ending the dramatic chase on the high seas. As we sailed further away from the pirate boats, everyone breathed a sigh of relief.

We headed south in the dark. The sea was relatively calm. The weary passengers now slumbered after a day of terror.

From a far distance, I saw a glow of amber light on the horizon. Was it the lights of a city, or an oil platform in the middle of the open sea? We decided to check it out.

Before daybreak, we reached an offshore oil platform with a large oil tanker anchored to it. We circled around the bright, illuminated scaffold-like structure. There was no one in sight.

"Help! Help!" I stood on top of the poop deck and yelled. There was no response.

At dawn, I saw a man dressed in a white uniform appear on the bridge high above the oil tanker.

"No smoke! No smoke!" he screamed and then asked, "What do you want?"

"We need help!" I replied.

"This is a tanker, you must stay away!"

"Can you give us some food and water?"

The man disappeared. Half an hour later, he returned and lowered a water hose and a bucket full of crackers and cookies.

"I have given you what you need, and now you must leave!" he shouted from the deck.

I thanked him for the badly-needed food supplies. At least there was enough to feed the starving children on board.

As we were about to turn away, there was a commotion in the front of the upper deck. An older lady had died of a heart attack. There was not much we could do, except cover her body with a blanket.

At the same time, a Malaysian naval patrol boat came out of nowhere and ordered us to stop. Two sailors came aboard. One of them seized the compass lying on the dashboard of the wheel room. (Someone hid the second compass in the engine room minutes before the sailor came aboard). The second sailor tied a rope to the bow of our boat.

Then I saw the captain of the patrol boat in a white uniform emerging from the bridge. He told me in Mandarin Chinese (possibly he was an ethnic Chinese) that we had violated Malaysian territory, and he was going to tow us to another location.

Again we were being towed at high speed out to the open sea. We did not have the slightest idea what they would do to us. Were they going to push us out to the high seas as they had done frequently to the other refugee boats they intercepted? As we continued the journey, the only compass on board indicated we were heading south. Possibly toward Singapore or Indonesia. At the very least, we would not have to worry about Thai pirates anymore.

I fell asleep on the floor of the wheel room, too tired to do anything. I woke up to find the boat had already stopped. Outside it was pitch dark. It was about three or four o'clock in the morning. I went up to the deck. A Malaysian sailor untied the tow rope and instructed us to sail toward the direction of the lighthouse high on a hilltop nearby. We thanked him. Then we headed in the direction of the gleaming light of the light house.

At sunrise, we were chugging along a chain of uninhabited greenish-colored islands. I was awed by the stunning beauty and surreal quietness of the surrounding scene under the morning sun. The crisp air, blue water and rugged islands with shorelines that dropped precipitously into the surrounding waters or with patches of idyllic white sand pristine beaches, were so inviting, yet there was not a living soul in sight.

This was truly a paradise! I wouldn't mind staying on these islands for the rest of my life. I sat on the poop deck, spellbound by the beauty around me.

"Tinh, Tinh," I heard someone calling my name. It was Skipper Xe who wanted to see me. I walked over to the wheel room.

"What are we going to do with the corpse of the lady who died on board?" Xe asked.

"I suppose we should dispose of it before we reach any port of entry." I assumed that bringing this to any seaport might raise suspicions of infectious disease and could subject us to quarantine or denial of entry. I sent Phat to express condolences to the bereaved family and discuss the burial. They were quite upset, yet reluctantly agreed to hold a funeral at sea.

Meanwhile, Phat was confronted by several angry passengers on the upper deck threatening that once the boat reached shore, they intended to beat up Skipper Xe and everyone else who was in charge. They accused us of incompetence, and blamed us for allowing the boat to be robbed by the pirates. Some even wanted to take revenge for the death of the older lady. I told Phat not to argue with them for the time being. The most urgent task was to deal with the dead body.

Immediately, we gathered a few helpers to assist with the funeral. After we carefully re-wrapped the body, we placed it on a piece of old plywood and tied two water containers to the bottom of it. A monk, who happened to be on board, performed a simple ritual and burned incenses. Then the improvised coffin was slowly lowered into the sea.

Boat PK3399 — Journey at Sea

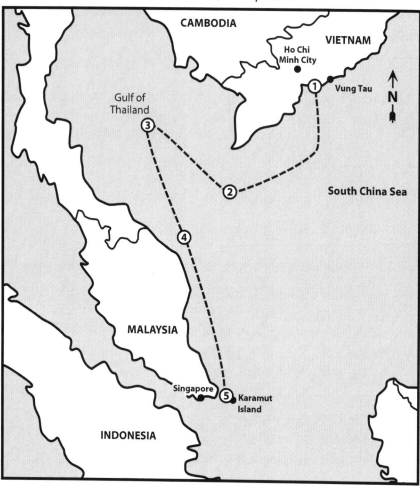

1) **June 4, 1979, afternoon:** Boat PK3399 departed Port 73, a small, make-shift pier along National Highway QL-51, 70 miles southeast of Ho Chi Minh City, Vietnam.

2) **June 6, 1979, midnight:** encountered Thai pirates in the South China Sea, robbed and then towed by pirates toward the Gulf of Thailand.

3) **June 7, 1979, morning:** robbed, again, by Thai pirates.

4) **June 8, 1979, morning:** intercepted by Malaysian Navy patrol, towed by patrol ship toward the south.

5) **June 9, 1979, morning:** safe arrival on Karamut Island, a remote islet of the Kepulauan Anambas Islands chain, Riau Islands Province, Indonesia.

– CHAPTER 5 –

Coming Ashore

The boat engine started again and we slowly chugged along the inlet between two chains of islands, looking for any human soul who would take us in.

"Someone is coming!" Soon I heard Phat yelling.

I looked toward the bow. A little sampan appeared around the corner of the island. As it got closer, I saw a dark-skinned man standing next to a blue plastic tarp in the middle of the sampan. A white and red flag was attached to a pole on the bow. Another man sat at the rear operating an outboard motor.

"Money… island," the man said in broken English as he pointed to the direction of another island.

I assumed he meant if we gave him money he would take us to an island.

"Singapore, Indonesia?" I pointed at the red and white flag. I first wanted to know which country we were in.

"Indonesia" he replied.

Now, everyone was excited and felt a sense of relief. We soon would stand on solid ground!

"How much?" I asked again.

"Three hundred dollars."

"Three hundred dollars? We do not have three hundred dollars," I said. "We were robbed three times on our way here."

Then I asked the people for help. Someone handed me a piece of gold jewelry and a twenty dollar bill. I gave it to the Indonesian. He nodded and told us to follow him.

We sailed for another hour to the other side of the island. From a distance I saw houses along the shoreline. Fishing boats and a wooden pier came into sight. As we approached, there were policemen and local officials already waiting for us at the pier. I got off the boat and followed them to the island's office.

A dark-skinned man in his forties, with a deformed leg, came to the front door to greet me.

"Welcome to Karamut Island," he spoke in English with a stern face. "I am the mayor of the island."

I told him that I was the representative of the boat.

"You need to pay a docking fee before everyone can get off the boat," he insisted.

I explained to him that we were robbed by Thai pirates and the boat was a mess. I promised to pay him once we got off the boat, and would give him whatever I could collect from the passengers.

"OK, this is the deal," he finally agreed. "I will allow your people to get off with one condition. You must pay within twenty four hours or I will push you out to sea."

"Yes, I promise," I replied.

On my way back to the boat I wondered, even though I had gained permission to disembark, how could I control the angry passengers who had threatened the crew? Besides, the pirates had turned every-thing on board upside down. Allowing everyone to search for his or her personal belongings could prove to be a disaster and any distur-bance on the overcrowded boat could easily cause it to flip over and capsize. I thought for a moment how I must control the situation until everyone got ashore safely.

"Listen, everyone!" I stood on the deck and announced a stern warning. "By order of the island police, everyone must get off the boat without carrying any belongings, and anyone who causes a disturbance on the boat or on shore shall be arrested and expelled from the island."

To my surprise, everyone followed my instructions to come ashore without any incident, including those troublemakers who had threatened the crew. Later that day, the crew unloaded every item and piled them up on a dock. One by one the passengers came forward to claim their personal belongings.

Karamut Island was a fishing village with a population of less than 100. There was only one small grocery store run by a Chinese woman. The villagers were kind enough to allow the newly-arrived visitors to stay overnight on the front porches of their houses. Some charged a small fee. Joyce bought several bags of instant noodles to cook for dinner. I found a nice, quiet corner of an abandoned warehouse by the dock. I spread a piece of plastic on the floor, large enough for seven of us to sleep on for the night. This was the first time we slept on solid ground in six days. Overnight, I still felt the ground floating as if we were still sailing on the high seas.

The next day I brought the docking fee I collected from the passengers to the village office. The mayor happily accepted it and told me he had arranged for the police to take us to a refugee camp on another island nearby.

That afternoon, we boarded the boat again for a one hour trip to Letung Island.

Letung was a commercial town in the Kepulauan Anambas Islands chain, part of Riau Islands Province, Indonesia. It was located 150 miles east of the Malaysian shores in the South China Sea. It became a transient port for the Vietnamese boat people and a food distribution center. When we arrived, there were already more than 30,000 refugees settling in the camps on three adjacent islands. Many stores lined both sides of the one small pier on the island to cater to the needs of refugees. There was no post office on the island. I met a store owner who acted as the mail carrier. He collected mail and delivered it to Tangjung Pinang, a main island nearby, for a hefty fee. On the day I arrived, I immediately sent a letter to Joyce's aunt in Hong Kong so that she could telegraph my father that we had safely arrived in Indonesia.

One morning I strolled down to the pier by myself. The marketplace was not yet open. There were only a handful of fishermen unloading their fresh catch. The boat PK3399 still docked idly at the far end of the pier. Soon it would be towed to another port for dismantling or salvage. I climbed aboard. The boat was empty except for a small pile of garbage stacked in the middle of the lower deck. I sat by myself on the poop deck where I had spent most of my time during the six-day journey. I looked toward the bow where the canvas top that covered the upper deck had been removed, leaving behind a wooden skeleton. The glossy green cabin and deck still shone brightly under the morning sun, as if she was proudly displaying her undeniable accomplishment.

There was no shelter for refugees on the island. Everyone either rented a place from the locals or slept in the open until the local authority designated a place for them to settle down. I found a cement slab on the front porch of a store behind the town square. It had a canvas awning as shelter from rain and the blazing sun. The store owner allowed my family to stay on the porch overnight. We had lost most of our belongings to the pirates. Only Joyce recovered a piece of gold leaf she hid inside the collar of her underwear. I took it to the store and exchanged it for about seven thousand Indonesian rupiahs (about 120 U.S. dollars). It would last several weeks if we only spent it on food.

On one hot afternoon, an Indonesian man walked by. He saw Joyce holding Irene, sitting under the shade of the front awning of the store. He introduced himself as the owner of the hotel next to the town square. He offered us a small space for ten dollars a month. We accepted his offer. The hotel was a run-down, two-story, wood frame building. The space we rented was a small corner next to the staircase on the upper level. It at least kept us out of the harsh elements until we could relocate to a refugee camp.

The hotel had no running water or toilets for guests. The only sanitation access on the island was the rocky beach. There was a public outhouse on the creek behind the hotel, but refugees were not allowed to use it. The town allowed refugees to get their water supply from a stream up the hill and to use the shower stalls nearby; one for men on the upper stream and the ladies took the lower one.

The population on this remote island was predominantly Indonesian Muslim. There was a local mosque behind the hotel where we were staying. Each morning I was awakened by the annoying blast from a loudspeaker hanging on an electrical pole in the square outside my window. Someone was chanting the Salah, the call for Morning Prayer. Some local residents were polite and hospitable because refugees brought tremendous business to the island. However, others were hostile to us — apparently the presence of refugees was intrusive to their laid-back lifestyle. One afternoon I had a stomach cramp, and I could not run to the rocky beach. Instead, I ran to the public outhouse behind the hotel. As I stepped out of the outhouse, several Indonesian men saw me. They chased me and threw stones at me. I ran up the hill and hid until dusk.

The United Nations High Commissioner for Refugees (UNHCR) warehouse was located next to the town square on the other side of the hotel. It stored relief-essential food supplies such as rice, oil, salt and eggs, etc. The food supply was supposedly distributed to the refugees. However, the Indonesian officials would sell them to the local market and pocket the profit. As for the refugees, they had no other choice but to buy the same food supply from the local merchants.

One hot afternoon, a rotten odor permeated the square. I walked to the UNHCR warehouse to find its door wide open. I saw the Indonesians in charge of the warehouse throwing rotten eggs and vegetables out onto the street. They would rather let the food rot in the warehouse rather than feed the starving refugees who had no money to buy food.

On the upper level of the hotel where we stayed, there lived a family of five people. The older son was in his twenties and his name was Thang. One day Thang asked me to join him in selling fish in the market. Instead of buying fish from the wholesalers by the pier, he went to the other side of the island to deal directly with the fishing boats that came ashore daily, for a better bargain.

So every morning before dawn we followed a winding trail in the darkness to the other side of the island and waited for the fishermen to come ashore with the freshest catch of the day. The daily run yielded a few hundred rupiahs, enough for us to buy vegetables for the day and to bring a few unsold fish home for dinner.

One morning we arrived at the beach earlier than usual, and instead of waiting for the boat to come ashore, Thang took a canoe and went out to meet the fishing boat. I was by myself, strolling along the deserted beach and watching the morning stars recess. The red and orange sun emerged like a fireball behind the dark clouds on the horizon. Its brilliant colors flickered on the wavering ocean water.

I watched the waves roll briskly in and out over the white sand beneath my feet. The bent coconut trees swayed gently in the morning breeze. The fresh, salty air caressed my face. It was calm and beautiful. I never thought I could be so alive to enjoy this breathtaking sunrise on an Indonesian beach.

I marveled at how I could have made it this far. Who am I? Nothing but a lowly person, insignificant and as small as a grain of sand that was under my feet. Yet the Creator of the universe, whom I trust, still cares for me to this day. His unfailing love and faithfulness surpasses all my understanding. His majesty and glory are far beyond the splendors of all His creations combined. I was awe-struck by the beauty of the awesome display before me. I felt compelled to drop to my knees on the wet sand. Gazing at the beautiful morning sky, I thanked God for His wondrous plan being revealed in my life.

Life was quite different from the grim war in the jungles of South Vietnam, from the fear of living under the communist regime, or from the horrors we faced when we were chased and robbed by pirates in the Gulf of Thailand. It was different now, simply because God provided strength and endurance for me to pursue what I have been longing for so many years — to live free.

I picked up a long wooden stick and wrote in the sand, large enough to be seen from the air: *live free, or die.*

Town square on Letung Island. The building on the right is the hotel where we stayed. Behind the hotel is the local mosque.

(Photo courtesy of Archive of Vietnamese Boat People)

– CHAPTER 6 –

Kuku Island

Three weeks later, the refugee office informed us that all passengers of boat PK3399 are to be settled in Kuku Refugee Camp, one of the three camps located in the Kepulauan Anambas Islands chain. While Joyce and Irene remained at the hotel until the lease expired, my brothers and I went to Kuku to begin building a straw hut large enough for the whole family. This would become our home for the next six months.

We arrived on Kuku Island one morning to find more than 1,000 refugees already settled along the beach. There was no food supply, no market place, no medical facility or even an outhouse. First, we bought timbers and straw from a local merchant. We built a bed out of wood planks large enough for the whole family. During our first night in the newly-built hut, a thunderstorm moved through the island. It rained so heavily that it turned the straw roof into a shower spout, but at least the wood frame was strong enough to sustain the gusts of wind. We put on raincoats and slept through the night. Within a week, Tony and his friends dug a well near the hut. The well water was clean enough for laundry and bathing, but we still had to boil the water for drinking. Soon we took in three other friends who could not find shelter to join us in the already crowded hut.

"Kuku" Island was supposedly a pristine and stunningly beautiful island. Bending coconut trees dotted the white sand beaches with a greenish-colored hill for the island's backdrop. It could well be a picture-perfect paradise if not for the swarms of flies that blackened all the food we prepared, the nauseating odor from open sewers, and the rampancy of diseases. The locals called it "the island of flies." The weather was always sizzling hot and humid and could easily reach up to 120 degrees by mid-day. It only cooled off late in the evening.

Two months after we landed at Kuku, more and more refugees arrived and the UNHCR established an office with a governing committee run by refugees. A well-equipped clinic with a medical team and surgical equipment was in place, including a five-bed inpatient ward and a helicopter pad on top of the hill for emergency medical evacuation. And finally, a food supply warehouse on the island distributed food directly to the refugees, bypassing the corrupt Indonesian officials in Letung. A water system using metal pipes diverted fresh water from a creek on the hill to the camp and a marketplace provided every necessity we wanted. Dozens of restaurants sprung up along the beach offering a variety of cuisine from Vietnamese spring rolls to french bread. The most notable improvement was the construction of two large outhouses by the beach — large enough to meet the need of more than 15,000 refugees at its height of capacity.

Soon after I arrived at Kuku Island, I met Pastor Tran Duc Toan who was an associate pastor of a Chinese Christian church in Ho Chi Minh City. He arrived at the camp in early June. Together we organized a Bible study group with more than two dozen Chinese and Vietnamese Christians in the camp. The meetings usually took place at homes or by the beach.

In early August, World Vision International sent a team to visit the camp. They brought in more than 200 New International Version (NIV) Bibles and provided several pieces of large blue tarp, as well as cash for nails and tools to build a chapel on the island. After the camp committee approved a lot on prime beachfront property for the chapel site, Pastor Toan mobilized a few Christian friends to collect wood beams and started the construction project. All the men did the construction work and the women prepared meals and drinks. We certainly had a lot of fun. After two weeks of hard work, an uncomplicated, yet practical, blue triangle-shaped chapel was completed. Inside was a raised stage with a podium and benches for seating more than 70 people, all made of timbers chopped down from the hills behind the camp. We took sand to smooth out the uneven floor and made the final touches for the dedication ceremony.

One beautiful Sunday morning we celebrated with joyful tears as we gathered to dedicate the new chapel. We offered thanksgiving for the freedom of worshipping God in a foreign land without the watchful eyes of secret police.

The small chapel on Kuku Island.
"Tin Lanh" means good news in Vietnamese.

Despite all the efforts, sanitation and health in such a crowded camp continued to be the main concern. The clinic had to cope with hepatitis, malaria, malnutrition and other diseases. In addition to the health problems we confronted each day, there was the tremendous heat, millions of flies, terrible odors and overcrowded housing. Death became so common in the camp that the temporary cemetery on the hillside was dotted with more than 100 makeshift graves in the short two months after I arrived. Mostly the dead were babies and young children. At the beginning, at least three to five children died each day of an unknown disease which caused high fever and diarrhea. They usually died within twenty four hours after the symptoms developed. The situation only began to improve as better hygiene and medical facilities started to function, providing the badly needed tools to fight against this stubborn killer.

Irene now had grown to be a little princess, lovely and healthy, rarely cranky or demanding. She had been through a lot more than other children at her age. We were so blessed to have her, a comfort and joy in time of trial. On her first birthday, Marvin bought a red apple as her birthday present, the only thing we could afford. My favorite part of each day was to take Irene to the beach and watch her play with her neighborhood friends, while staying under the shade of coconut trees and enjoying the sea breeze in the heat of the day.

One hot afternoon we came to our usual spot at the beach to find that one of Irene's little friends did not show up. Later we were shocked to learn she had died overnight of the unknown disease. Fear began to grasp the camp and parents tried to isolate their children. But this did not do much good because we all lived in cramped and overcrowded huts.

Our next door neighbor, Tan Lam, was a former vice-president of a commercial bank in Saigon before the communists took over in 1975. He escaped by boat with his wife and two beautiful young teenage daughters and landed on Kuku at the same time we set foot on the island. Apparently they were some of the few lucky ones who were not robbed by pirates. They decorated their little straw hut with beautiful furniture and enjoyed exquisite French cuisine every day. Each time as they prepared their fresh meals, the smell of their cooking permeated the stinky air in the neighborhood. We all envied what they had on their table, and sometimes it made everyone lose their appetite for the canned fish we had to eat every day. They apparently enjoyed their stay in the camp as if they were vacationing on the island.

One early morning I was awakened by commotion from Tan Lam's hut. His oldest daughter had developed a high fever and was in a coma. Joyce went over to help them take her to the clinic. By midmorning, she died of an unknown illness. Her body had turned dark and the medical team could not determine what the cause was. The camp sent a team to bury the body and sprayed pesticide around the huts to prevent the virus from spreading.

When we first set foot on Kuku Island, most of us assumed we might stay no more than three months before we could resettle in another country. However, as more and more refugees arrived at the camp every day, few countries would come to the camp for resettlement interviews. I realized it was unlikely that UNHCR could process such a large number of people any time soon.

As we anticipated a longer stay in the camp and our meager savings had been depleted, Marvin and I decided to teach English to earn some money to put food on the table. We taught four classes each day with more than 40 students in attendance. With the decent income, we now could afford bread, fresh meat, and vegetables — things we had not tasted for a long time.

Life in the refugee camp was uneventful, yet never boring. Our daily routine was chopping firewood up the hill for cooking, then standing in long lines for food. The lucky ones had their names called to the office for resettlement interviews. The hope in everyone's mind was that someday they could leave this overcrowded, disease-infested island for good.

The only excitement in the camp was when visitors came to the island. We flocked to them with thousands of letters (without stamps) in the hope that they were kind enough to mail them for us. There was not much going on in the camp after dark, except for the camp PA system blasting contemporary music and *Cai Luong* (South Vietnamese Opera) and a few announcements in between. Once in a while the camp office organized a live show or contest. Contestants were selected from among the refugees. The entertainment had brought some fun, or perhaps revived a ray of hope to the 15,000 desperate refugees who had no idea what their future would be like.

Kuku Island today. The heap of rocks on the right was the site where we built the chapel on the island.

(Photo courtesy of Archive of Vietnamese Boat People)

– CHAPTER 7 –

Horror at Sea

One evening I went to visit my friend Lin at his little hut. I saw a man in his forties sitting on a bench by the window. His skin was dark under the flickers of the candlelight. An oversized white shirt apparently enveloped his frail and skinny body.

"He is a newcomer, and his name is Tran," Lin said as he poured me a cup of water. "Someone brought him to the island a couple of days ago. He has no relatives or friends, so I took him in."

Lin sat down next to me. He told me Tran's story, one that I will never forget.

Tran was the owner of an export and import business in Saigon before the communists took over in 1975. Like many Chinese ethnic merchants, Tran's wealth was all but wiped out under the new regime. However, with his connections, he organized a fishing boat to set sail from My Tho, a seaport near the Mekong Delta. On board were his parents, wife, children, relatives and 200 other passengers. As they approached a Malaysian island and prepared to land, they were intercepted and denied entry by a Malaysian Navy patrol boat. As the patrol boat pushed Tran's overcrowded boat back out to sea, the boat's bow cracked open and threw everyone into the roaring waves. Tran was the sole survivor because he was an excellent swimmer and the only person rescued by the patrol boat. As he lay restlessly on the deck gasping for air, he saw only debris floating by. There was no sign of life. He said he was too exhausted to jump back into the sea, but that he would rather die with his family than to live a life without them.

For most of the time, Tran stared into the void of darkness outside his hut, and only turned to respond with a few words and a hollow expression of resignation and despair. It was as if his will to survive had been snuffed out of his soul.

Walking through the dark alley on my way home, I pondered and blamed the distant evil communist regime for pushing this man and thousands of others like he and I out to sea. Only the lucky ones landed on this island and other refugee camps in Indonesia, Malaysia, Singapore, Philippines, Thailand and Hong Kong. Most refugees have their own horror stories to tell and accounts of someone who had not survived the ordeal.

There is no official figure of how many boat people had escaped Vietnam or how many had perished. According to the UN Refugee Commission's estimate, there were 930,000 boat people who safely arrived in refugee camps. Conservative estimates state that 250,000 boat people died at sea, a figure almost equivalent to the total of South Vietnamese civilian casualties in the entire Vietnam War (1959-1975). Some say that as many as 50 percent of the refugees who escaped from Vietnam subsequently perished at sea. No matter the number, however, the human suffering was unimaginably horrible.[1]

The majority of deaths were caused by overcrowded and ill-prepared, rickety boats that succumbed to the horrible weather. Many boats left at the height of the monsoon season. Some of the boats broke into pieces before they even departed from their port of origin. Many also had engine problems at sea and drifted on for weeks and even months.

Though the casualties among the boat people were disastrous, some of the stories of those who survived were even more horrifying. Many had to do with the Thai pirates. An estimated 60 percent of refugee boats that sailed in or near the Gulf of Thailand were attacked by pirates. The pirates also set out in search of innocent prey in the South China Sea, and often found it. I heard bone-chilling tales of cruel and barbaric acts committed by professional Thai pirates. Apparently, once they boarded the boat, they ransacked the boat and robbed the escapees. Men were clubbed or knifed and thrown overboard, and a few others were kept as slaves. Women were repeatedly raped and tortured with savagery beyond imagination. Some were sold as sex slaves to brothels in Thailand. I met a few women in Kuku camp who were victimized by these pirates. One carried the baby to full term. Another woman could not bear the humiliation and took her own life.

After the robberies, the pirates would sometimes destroy the engine and leave the boat adrift at sea for months. A lucky few were allowed to continue their journey and finally arrived in refugee camps. I considered myself and others on boat PK3399 fortunate among the refugees. Though the amateur pirates had stripped us of our possessions, at least they allowed us to continue the journey and safely come ashore in one piece.

Was it worth it to escape Vietnam for the sake of freedom? When I posed this question to the refugees I talked to in the camp, almost always the answer was a definite "yes." However, when I asked if they would do it again by boat with what they had been through, without hesitating their response was almost always "no." One older man put it in a proper perspective: "I would rather fight against the communists until I die, than perish in the roaring sea."

Why would these people abandon everything they owned, uproot themselves from the country they once called home for generations, to embark on a journey of no return with an uncertain future and significant risk of death?

A vast majority of the boat people who set out to sea were ethnic

Chinese. The ethnic Chinese had settled in Vietnam, mostly in Cho Lon, as early as the French colonial period (1880-1940). They maintained a high degree of autonomy and were protected by the French colonial authority. After the country had declared independence in 1954, and later partitioned into North and South Vietnam, the South Vietnamese government allowed the ethnic Chinese to keep the same rights as the indigenous people. With hard work and business expertise, they enjoyed privilege and economic prosperity in the country the locals called "The Land of Plentiful Rice and Fish." The Chinese in Vietnam controlled 70 percent of the economy of South Vietnam prior to 1975.

Despite owning large resources, the wealthy Chinese in South Vietnam rarely contributed to the local community with the exception of building a few schools and hospitals. Needless to say, when the war effort against the communist invasion during the Vietnam War began, the Chinese in South Vietnam contributed little to the call. When their children were to be drafted into the ARVN, the rich Chinese would pay bribes so their loved ones could stay in the rear bases or to buy a deferment from the service. Only the poor, like me, had no other choice but to be sent to the battlefront. Some deserted from the horrors of the battlefield and returned home to hide from the military police. Others paid a large sum to sneak out of the country on cargo ships. Not only that, a few wealthy ethnic Chinese businessmen even secretly provided financial support to the Viet Cong insurgency in order to protect their own business interests. Others were brainwashed to join ranks with a communist underground organization called "Hoa Van" (Chinese Movement) to undermine the South Vietnam government and extort money from ethnic Chinese merchants.

After "unifying" the country in 1976, the Hanoi communist regime intended to minimize the century-old influence from their powerful neighbor to the north. They imposed an anti-capitalist policy in 1978 which obviously afflicted the majority of the ethnic Chinese population in the country. Soon relations with China turned sour due to the resentment toward the ethnic Chinese. Vietnam accused China of inciting the ethnic Chinese to rebel. In response, China cut off all aid and supported the Cambodian Khmer Rouge regime in an attack on the Vietnam's southwestern provinces. In March of 1979, China invaded North Vietnam.

As these events unfolded, the ethnic Chinese in South Vietnam began to realize they were the target of revenge. All the wealth they had accumulated for generations vanished overnight. Many were imprisoned or kicked out of their own homes. Those ethnic Chinese who once supported the Viet Cong insurgency, or who had become members of the Hoa Van during the war, were not immune from the vengeance. Many were arrested and put in prisons in order to prevent them from engaging in subversive activities. Despite this, China had no desire to take any ethnic Chinese back, leaving them with only one alternative — the sea.

What if the Chinese in South Vietnam had been actively involved in fighting against the communist invasion instead of supporting them? Could there have been a different outcome to the Vietnam War? Given the nature of the conflict, it was critical to inform and win the hearts and souls of the people of South Vietnam. Without bribery, there would have been fewer corrupt officials and military officers and more motivated leaders in the South Vietnamese government. Without financial support for the Viet Cong insurgency, their already shabby political infrastructure in the south would eventually collapse.

Nevertheless, one thing I learned from this painful lesson is that the freedom we enjoy today does not come without a price. Our corollary problem is that we often take it for granted and do not realize we are free because others had paid the heavy price for us. Even to this day we have become so accustomed to the freedom we enjoy that we may not be able to defend it when it is in jeopardy.

– CHAPTER 8 –

Galang Refugee Camp

December 10, 1979, while I was busy preparing for the first Christ-mas celebration at the Seaside Chapel, I got called to the camp office.

"So, you are Daniel Luc?" asked Mr. Thong who was in charge the refugee resettlement. (The UN resettlement program allows refugees to change their names if they wish.)

"Yes," I answered.

"You and your family are going to Canada," he said.

"What do you mean Canada? It must be a mistake. I never applied to immigrate to Canada," I said. I was puzzled. "I only applied to go to the United States, New Zealand, or Australia. Besides, I don't even have any relative in Canada who could sponsor me."

"I don't know. That is what this document indicates." He handed the document to me.

"Can I reject it?"

"No, the UN has made the decision that any delay will void your privilege of resettlement in any country," he continued. "You must report to the pier and travel to Galang for the immigration process."

I told Joyce, Marvin and my other brothers. They all agreed that I should go and take Jason with me.

The next afternoon, Joyce, Irene, Jason and I packed some cloth-ing, said farewell to friends and left this once unpopulated, beautiful paradise behind. On one hand, I was excited that my life as a refugee soon would come to an end. It was only a matter of going through the immigration process and then my family and I would resettle in a new country. On the other hand, my heart was burdened with so many desperate friends that I would be leaving behind, not knowing how long it would be before they found a better future in a new country.

We boarded a UN chartered cargo ship. After 16 hours sailing through a ghostly dark sea, we arrived at Galang refugee camp on a rainy morning.

Galang Island is located near the equator southeast of Singapore, one of more than 1700 islands in the Riau Archipelago region. Unlike the tropical islands resting peacefully nearby, one half mile from the pier and over the beautiful green pristine rolling hills was the temporary home, at one point in time, for more than 20,000 Vietnamese refugees. The UN set up Galang Refugee Camp in 1979 as a refugee processing center to accommodate the influx of Vietnamese boat people. Most of the refugees arriving at Galang were transferred from other islands for the immigration process. It was the only transit point, perhaps the only gateway of hope, for thousands of refugees who dreamed of a better life in a country they never knew.

Galang was a well-organized and well-established refugee camp thanks to the efforts of the UNHCR. It had many barrack-style dwellings and facilities such as a camp administrative and a resettlement office, an Indonesian police station, a well-equipped hospital, and the office and living quarters for the UNHCR officials. When I first arrived, the construction of a new gravel road leading from the pier to the heart of the camp had started. More and more buildings and barracks sprung up over the hilly landscape in order to meet the increasing demand of refugees who arrived daily.

We were assigned to a barrack in Camp II, one of many single-story buildings situated on a slope. Each barrack could accommodate approximately 40 people. The barrack was constructed with a wood frame over a concrete slab covered with corrugated metal roofing. There were double-stack wooden bunk beds lined up on both sides of the room creating a center aisle with three florescent lights dangling from the ceiling. At one end of the barrack was a shower stall, and every two barracks shared a stand-alone kitchen shed. By midday, the temperature inside the barrack was unbearably hot. Yet it was still, by far, better conditions than the straw huts on Kuku Island.

The next day we went to the resettlement office. To our disappointment the Canadian team had gone home for Christmas break and would not return to Galang until mid-January. We had to wait.

On January 10, my name was announced on the PA system and that I must come to the resettlement office for an interview by the U.S. delegation. I was quite surprised and confused.

"Mr. Luc, where have you been?" the U.S. team leader named Mary asked. "We have been looking all over the refugee camps for you!"

"Madam, I have been in the Galang camp for almost a month." I answered politely.

"Who told you to come here?"

"The UN officials sent us here. They said my family and I were supposed to go to Canada." I handed the transfer document to her.

"No, no. You must come to United States!" She paused for a moment as she reviewed the document.

"A church in Chicago has sponsored you and your family. Since your brother Alex Luc is now a U.S. citizen and because of your affiliation with the U.S. military during the war, we are proud to welcome you to the United States of America."

"Thank you! But, what about going to Canada?" I asked.

"Don't worry. I've already taken care of it," she assured me. "Besides, since we need someone to manage the resettlement office, would you mind helping us?"

"Sure, I would be happy to." I replied.

So for the next three months, while I waited for the completion of my immigration process, I worked in the resettlement office. My daily task was to help organize the screening and interview sessions by delegations from various countries. It was the least I could contribute to meeting the increasing needs of the refugee camp.

One day the Australian team came to me for help. Since I had been a military interpreter, they wanted me to interview several "people of interest," particularly two individuals who had been at the camp since it opened its doors. Both were former members of the Vietnamese Labor (Communist) Party and high ranking officers in the Hanoi regime. Because of their background, no country would allow them political asylum for fear of repercussion. My job was to obtain information surrounding their defection. The Australian government would not mind granting them asylum and a chance to settle in a free nation if they met their requirements.

Nguyen Van Nam was born in the Mekong Delta region, South Vietnam. As a young recruit of the Viet Minh Movement, he was regrouped (Tap Ket) to the North in 1954 after the Geneva Accord partitioned North and South Vietnam. In 1960, Nam was part of the NLF army units that moved south on Ho Chi Minh Trail to participate in the armed struggle against "American Imperialism." He joined the 1968 Tet Offensive and later took part in the final assaults to overthrow the South Vietnamese government in 1975. He then was promoted to the rank of major in the North Vietnamese Army.

Thinking that the victory would bring peace and independence to his native land once and for all, he never thought his dream would be crushed just a little more than a year after the war ended. In July 1976, when South and North Vietnam finally unified, Nam retired from the army. Like many of his comrades from the south, he was no longer allowed to hold any prominent position in the new government. His

new position was a manager of a small government-owned food supply company near Ho Chi Minh City.

He felt betrayed by those he had served with in the NLF organization. Seeing the country in shambles after the communist regime took
over the south, he had lost faith in the socialist system and the future
of the country for which he had been fighting for his whole life. He
decided to flee the country with his wife and two children. His family
had been at the refugee camp since the first day it opened, but he had
been unable to find a country that would take him in.

The second person was Tran Cam Thu. Thu was a Saigoner in his
late thirties. He joined the NLF when he was fifteen years old and
spent a few years studying in high school in Ha Noi. Later he joined
the Vietnamese Labor Party. After graduating from college, he became
a NLF diplomat to the communist bloc countries in Eastern Europe.
Thu returned to his native city a year after the South was "liberated,"
and reunited with his parents and relatives.

Soon he discovered that people in the south were not starving or
enslaved by the South Vietnamese regime. He realized that what the
North Vietnamese had alleged about the suffering under American
Imperialism in the South was a total lie. His parents had a successful business and owned a beautiful home. When the new government
imposed the Purge and Inventory Campaign, his parents' business
and home became a target. They all lost their possessions. However, because their son was a high-ranking government official, they
were considered a "revolutionary family," and were allowed to stay in
Saigon.

Thu assumed his contribution to the NLF would earn him a higher
position in the new government once he returned. To his dismay, he
was assigned to a district level position in the city doing administrative work. His superior was a northerner who had powerful political
clout with the central government.

Upset by what he had seen, and feeling ashamed for what his parents had to suffer under the new regime, he and his wife escaped by boat and arrived at the Galang refugee camp.

There were other former communist government officials who also defected and stayed in the camps. Some openly admitted their background while others' identities were disclosed by someone who happened to know them. Despite all of this, they were treated equally and surprisingly well. There was no animosity toward them in the camp.

As for Nguyen Van Nam and Tran Cam Thu (I am not sure these were their real names), they still were in the camp when I left Galang.

On March 20, 1980, after three months of waiting, physical check-ups, and more waiting, we were finally granted a visa to migrate to the United States. Joyce, Irene, Jason and I took a six-hour boat trip to Singapore and temporarily stayed at a former military barracks in Sembawang where we prepared for a flight to America.

We spent one week in Singapore. We used our rationed money for bus rides to explore the clean and beautiful city. The people were polite and helpful despite our less-than-desirable appearance. Some bus drivers even allowed us to ride free when we ran out of cash. The most memorable moment was having a bowl of Hainanese chicken rice at the hawker center in downtown Singapore. We had not had such a delicious meal in the past nine months. I finally realized I was back in the civilized world, leaving behind all the painful memories and injustices. I was eagerly looking forward to facing the challenges of rebuilding my future in America.

On March 26, we boarded an airplane that took us to Hong Kong. I quickly contacted my aunt and Joyce's uncles. They came to see us at the hotel where we stayed overnight. They were shocked to see us dressed in worn-out clothing and sandals and immediately took us out to shop for new clothes. They even found me a new pair of eyeglasses. The next day, as we were getting ready to board the flight to leave for the United States, my aunt handed me a twenty dollar bill. It was the only thing we had, apart from the clothing on our backs, to start our new life in the land of the free and the home of the brave — the United States of America.

By the pier at Galang Refugee Camp, March 1980.
L.-r.: Andrew, Daniel, Irene, Joyce, Jason and Marvin.

Epilogue

Reunited

On September 15, 1979, a little less than two months after seven of us arrived at Kuku Refugee Camp in Indonesia, a local public security agent named Dong came to the house where my parents and two other brothers (Benson and Thomas) were staying in Cho Lon, Vietnam. He questioned my parents about my illegal activities involving the Boat PK3399 and the disappearance of their six children and one grandchild. By that time, anyone involved in organizing boats to leave the country were charged with committing subversive activity, and many had been arrested and sentenced to prison. At first my father stated he had no idea of our whearabouts. Dong kept threatening and harassing my parents, conducting searches of their house day and night. Finally my father told him we had fled the country and, since were all grown up, he had no control over our decision. However, Dong would not give up. Instead, he demanded a monthly payment of at least 1,000 piasters or he would charge my father as a reactionary, which could easily put him in prison.

My parents had used up most of their lifetime savings to pay for our trip out of Vietnam. With no more income, what they had left would barely last for another year. In order to keep this racketeering policeman silent, my father had to pay whatever he demanded. So when we resettled in another country, we were able to send the money home. This constant threat lasted until February 6, 1986. On that day, my parents and my brothers, Benson and Thomas, left Vietnam on a flight under the Orderly Departmet Program (ODP), a humanitarian program aimed to provide safe and orderly passage for Vietnamese refugees immigrating to the United States. The ODP was established at the end of 1979 under the auspices of the United Nations High Commissioner for Refugees. As for my parents, it ended years of horror and suffering under a totalitarian regime. They were finally reunited with their children whom they dearly loved.

Reunion

When I arrived in Chicago in the early 1980s, I shared my story with American friends and acquaintances. Their response to anything about the Vietnam War was negative and sometimes resentful. A few even advised me not to talk about it. Furthermore, I felt shocked to learn how the American Vietnam War veterans were being treated when they returned home. They were called "baby killers," "war-mongers" and were even spat on as they got off the airplane. They carried the scars of war home with them only to find themselves psychologically wounded again, unable to share their pain with anyone, even their closest family members. I was even more disgusted because I had fought alongside these veterans for six years, and witnessed what they had been through on the battlefield.

Whether Americans resented the war effort or felt ashamed at the outcome of the war, their anger should not have been directed toward the veterans who followed the call and faithfully served their country. The treatment they received from their fellow Americans, as far as I was concerned, was much worse than the way the Viet Cong treated their prisoners of war. Indeed, the debt we owe the American soldiers can never be adequately paid.

I tried to voice my concerns, or at least to tell the truth about the conflict. Who would listen to a guy like me talk about a war they were trying to ignore and forget?

In 1972, after Maj. Davidson flew back to the states, I was told by his colleagues that he was admitted to the hospital for mental treatment. They advised me not to contact him. Capt. Wanat had been confined in a NVA POW camp in Cambodia for ten months. I assumed his condition would have been much worse. I refrained from searching for them, or talking to anyone about them.

Things began to change in the mid-1980s. Although there weren't any welcome-home parades, or public recognition of the sacrifices these veterans had made or apologies for the ill treatment they received, the American public had come to grips with the reality of the war, and finally put the tragedy behind them to let the healing begin.

Twenty years have passed since I arrived in America. I often wondered what Maj. Thomas "Drew" Davidson and Capt. George Wanat, Jr., had been doing since they returned home. Were they able to build a new life? Or were they traumatized by the experiences other Vietnam War Veterans had suffered? I wanted to find them but I was afraid my presence might stir up their painful memories and emotion.

I was not sure what I was supposed to do until one day in the summer of 2001, I was searching the internet and found a "people-search" website. I typed in "Thomas Davidson," and a list of more than twenty names appeared. I sorted through the list and compiled a shorter list based on my assumptions of where Maj. Davidson could be now. I recalled that, based on his accent, Maj. Davidson might be from one of the southern states. However, 29 years after we walked out of the jungle in Vietnam together for the last time, many things could have changed. Was he still alive? Would he remember me? Even if he did, would he talk to me? Nevertheless, I decided to find out in order to put closure on this chapter of my life.

Saturday morning, August 18, 2001, I sat on the front porch of my house and dialed the first phone number listed on a piece of scrap paper.

"Hello," a man answered the phone.

"Good morning, I'm trying to locate a person named Thomas Davidson."

"I am Thomas Davidson." His tone seemed hesitant.

"Hi, Mr. Davidson, can I ask you few questions?" I tried to be polite. I was afraid he was going to hang up on me.

"Go ahead."

"I'm looking for a Thomas Davidson who was in the Army?"

"Yes, I was in the Army. Go on."

"A major in the Army?"

"I was a major."

"Did you serve with Military Advisory Team 47 in An Loc, Vietnam, in April 1972?"

"So far, you know an awful lot about me. Just who in the hell are you anyway, and what do you want?"

"My name is Daniel Luc —"

"I never knew anyone named Daniel Luc!"

"*Thieu Ta* (Major), I am Sgt. Tinh, your interpreter." I said.

There was a moment of silence at the other end of the line.

"Oh, my God! The Lord is so good to me!" I heard him scream loudly at the other end of the line. "Are you Sgt. Tinh?"

"Yes!" I could not contain my emotions. I never thought this day would come. It was not a dream — I had finally found my lost friend.

"Sgt. Tinh, I have been searching for you all these years, but you have found me today. Oh, my God!" He was overjoyed.

We had an excited conversation that morning. He told me after he had come back to the United States in April 1972, he was admitted to a hospital for some sort of gastroenteritis. Most likely it was caused by the filthy water we drank in the jungle during the escape. I, also, had suffered something similar and it took me three months to recover. He reunited with his family in Tennessee and spent a year in Germany before retiring from the Army. He went back to school to get his law degree, became an attorney and practiced law in Tennessee. He has two sons. His older son, David, followed in his father's steps and became an army officer. His younger son was an engineer.

Two years earlier, his beloved wife died of cancer. The loss truly devastated him. A year later, he suffered a heart attack and went through bypass surgery. During his recovery at the hospital, he asked his son David to search for me. Trying to locate someone behind the iron curtain in Vietnam is like searching for a needle in a haystack. First, Drew had lost his beloved wife, and now his health was deteriorating. He felt life was no longer worth living. No one imagined that the day I called him would become the turning point of his life.

We chatted for almost an hour and agreed to plan for a reunion celebration. This was one of the happiest days of my life. What's more, I felt relieved to know he was not ill-affected as much by the war as many other Vietnam War veterans.

After we hung up the phone, Drew went to a wedding reception for one of his close friends. At the reception he met his high school sweetheart, Cathie. Six months later they got married. In one day, he had found his old friend and his future wife. "What a wonderful day! The Lord is so good to me," he later told me. His joyful voice still rings in my memory.

Four months later, on their way to England to attend a ceremony for his son David's promotion, Drew and Cathie and his sister-in-law stopped over in Chicago. Our first reunion in the terminal at O'Hare International Airport was short, yet emotional and exciting. There was no fanfare or publicity as I preferred to keep it between us. In the fall of 2006, I took a trip to Tennessee to visit Drew and meet his family and friends. Drew and I spent hours talking about the experience we encountered during the ordeal. He said it was the first time he could open up and share his experience since his return. No one else could understand the pain we both had endured.

October 2006 reunion at the Davidson's home, Lewisburg, Tennessee
(L.-r.): Daniel, Joyce, Cathie and Drew

Searching for Capt. George Wanat was a different story. I took finding Drew as a good sign, so I decided to look for George the next day.

I called George's phone number listed on a website. A lady answered the phone. She was George's mother. I told her I was looking for George Wanat, Jr., and explained about our encounter during the war.

"Mr. Luc, I beg you to call him right away." She was sincere and then she gave me another phone number listed in Massachusetts.

George answered the phone. He was surprised that I called. He spoke hesitantly to me, occasionally weeping throughout the conversation. I tried not to bring up anything about the past and tried to focus more on his present condition. Nevertheless, he was bitter and angry about how he was treated by the enemy as a prisoner, and was more resentful for his horrible experiences in the war. He was severely depressed and withdrawn. He told me he could not sleep most nights and had not been able to hold a job since the day he returned. He prayed often, and he still trusted the Lord would lead him through, but he felt his life was in ruins.

No one can fathom the pain and anguish these prisoners of war had to endure and suffer. The torture, humiliation, chains and cages, punishment, hunger and despair are more than most people can handle. I could not find a word to comfort or encourage him. All I could do was pray with him before I hung up the phone.

One month later I called him again. I asked if he would mind if I came to visit him. He hesitated without giving me an answer. Three months later I called again. The phone kept ringing. There was no answer. I have searched the internet, and have friends looking for him, but to no avail.

I still have not given up and I hope someday I can meet him again.

Life is sometimes like an intricate puzzle, beyond our comprehension. All three of us came from different parts of the world. We converged together upon a battlefield and faced the fiercest and most horrific fighting of the entire Vietnam War. Each of us came out of the war a different person. Nevertheless, we all have found one thing in common through this journey — God is still sovereign and faithful.

Return

As this book was about to be sent to the publisher, Joyce and I found ourselves on our way back to Vietnam. We had both retired and decided to spend three weeks traveling in Vietnam from north to south, Hanoi to Saigon (Ho Chi Minh City), visiting friends and relatives and seeing places we had never been able to visit. This was my second return trip since we fled the country 33 years ago. The first time was in 1996, the year our daughter Irene graduated from high school.

For years I struggled over whether I should return to An Loc and Loc Ninh. On one hand, I wanted to see how much had changed since I left but, on the other hand, I didn't want to stir up all the horrible, painful memories of my past. In the end, my curiosity trumped my fear. On May 21, 2012, Joyce and I hired a passenger van, left Ho Chi Minh City, and headed north on Highway QL-13.

The road once called "Mine Alley" had become a four-lane, asphalt-paved highway. Slowly, we drove past Chon Thanh and An Loc. The land on both sides of the road that I remembered as vacant and overgrown with tall weeds was now occupied by stores, houses, and industrial parks. Everything had changed. I didn't recognize any structure, building or street, much less anyone I knew who would still live in the area. I was told many of the residents were new settlers from another part of the country.

We continued to travel north toward Loc Ninh on QL-13. The red dirt road was undergoing major repairs and the drive was rough with potholes everywhere. The bumpy ride brought back many horrifying memories of the fighting along this stretch of the road during the war. But now it was so peaceful and surreal, and it felt strange not to be watching for landmines on the shoulder of the road or for sniper shots from the woods.

It didn't take me long to locate the Loc Ninh airfield. The abandoned runway was now a long strip of red dirt, a wasteland sandwiched between two rows of rubber trees, mostly covered with weeds and debris. The military compound next to the airstrip where I was once stationed is now long gone. In its place stands row after row of rubber trees. The old rustic entrance gate, the only remnant of the past, stood alone by the roadside. Nearby was a yellowish-colored war monument with a cement plaque near the bottom with words engraved in Vietnamese: "The central government has dedicated this plot of land as a historical landmark." The monument did not indicate what significant historical event had taken place there.

Loc Ninh Airfield entrance gate, May 2012.
The area between the rubber trees behind the gate was the airstrip.

I looked around the downtown area. Business in Loc Ninh was booming — its markets teeming with fresh goods and plenty of shoppers. The lives of the local residents seemed to have improved significantly. Many new housing developments were under construction on both sides of the road and up the hill. I couldn't see any scars of the war. I found the only memories from my time in Loc Ninh stored up in a small war museum down the slope. The museum displayed many war trophies and declared the North Vietnamese "liberation victories." Only a few residents there had any recollection of the battle of Loc Ninh. It was apparent that all they wanted was to put the past behind them and move forward toward a better future.

I felt the same way. I would like to end that chapter of my life with this book and move on with my life in the United States. However, from time to time, the scene of that beautiful sunrise returns in this old mind.

I will never forget the morning, 33 years ago, while I was living in the refugee camp on the island of Letung, Indonesia. I strolled along the white sand beach by myself, and gazed at the red and orange sun which was as radiant as a fireball behind the dark clouds over the horizon. Its brilliant colors flickered on the wavering ocean water as the waves briskly rolled in and out over the white sand beneath my feet. The bent coconut trees gently swayed in the morning breeze and the fresh, salty air caressed my face. It was so calm and beautiful. That morning I promised myself I would never forget what I have gone through, what costs I had paid in order to be free. In commemoration of my journey to freedom, I took a long, wooden stick and wrote these words in the sand at my feet: *live free, or die.*

Though my writing in the sand had been quickly washed away by the rising tides that morning, my will to live free will never diminish, just as many others in bondage and oppression will continue to search and struggle for freedom.

Endnotes

PART 1

Chapter 2

1) Vietnam War – Wikipedia, the free encyclopedia,
   http://en.wikipedia.org/wiki/Vietnam_War
2) What European country was entrenched in region
   before the U.S., http://answers.yahoo.com/question/
   index?qid=20080410102700AA8ev7M
3) The Binh Xuyen: Order and Opium in Saigon,
   http://www.drugtext.org/library/books/McCoy/book/28.htm
4) Ngo Dinh Nhu – Wikipedia, the free encyclopedia. (n.d.).
   Retrieved from http://en.wikipedia.org/wiki/Ngo_Dinh_Nhu

Chapter 3

1) Chicago: U. S. History Review: Chapter 30, The Vietnam War
   Years 1954; http://rkahr.blogspot.com/2008/03/chapter-30.html
   (accessed November 4, 2011).

Chapter 10

1) Ellithorpe, Harold, "Can you hold on just eight more minutes?"
   LIFE Magazine, 21 April 1972.

Chapter 13

1) Howard, John D., Brig. Gen., *The War We Came To Fight: A Study
   of the Battle of An Loc, April – June, 1972.*

2) Hollingsworth, James F., Maj. Gen., "Communist Invasion in Military Region III," unpublished narrative, 1972 (Microfiche Reel 44, Univeristy Publications of America: Records of the Military Assistance Command, Vietnam), p. 9.

3) Thi, Lam Quang, *Hell in An Loc, the 1972 Easter Invasion and the Battle that Saved South Vietnam*, p.150

4) Clark, Philip C., "The Battle That Saved Saigon," *Reader's Digest* March 1973.

Chapter 15

1) Chicago: Fall of Saigon – Wikipedia, the free encyclopedia, http://en.wikipedia.org/wiki/Fall_of_Saigon (accessed November 2, 2011).

PART TWO

Chapter 7

1) VietKa – Archives of Vietnamese Boat People, http://www.vietka.com/Vietnamese_Boat_People/HorribleStatistics.htm (retrieved 2010-12-11).

Abbreviations

AA	Anti-aircraft gun
ARVN	Armed Forces of Republic of Vietnam
AWOL	Absence without leave
CBU	Cluster Bomb Unit
COL	Colonel
CORDS	Civil Operations and Rural Development Support
CPT	Captain
FAC	Forward Air Controller
FSB	Fire Support Base
Gen.	General
KIA	Killed in action
Lt.	Lieutenant
LTC	Lieutenant Colonel
LTL	Lien Tinh Lo (Inter-Province Highway)
MACCORDS	Military Assistance Command and Civil Operations and Rural Development Support
MACV	Military Assistance Command Vietnam
Maj.	Major
MIA	Missing in action
MR3	Military Region 3
NCO	Non-commissioned Officer
NLF	National Liberation Front

NVA	North Vietnamese Army (aka VPA Vietnamese People's Army)
ODP	Orderly Departure Program
PF	Popular Force
POW	Prisoner of War
QL	*Quoc Lo* (National Highway)
R & R	Rest and Recuperation
RF	Regional force
SFC	Sergeant First Class
Sgt.	Sergeant
TOC	Tactical Operations Center
TRAC	Third Regional Assistance Command
UN	United Nation
UNHCR	United Nation High Commissioner for Refugees
VC	Viet Cong (Vietnamese Communist)
WIA	Wounded in action
WWII	World War II

Index

M

M-16 Rifle *59, 65, 66, 80, 84, 85*
M-60 machine gun *120*
M72- Light Anti-Tank Weapon *126*
Ma Quang *179, 180, 181, 182, 183, 184*
MACCORDS (Military Assistance
  Command and Civil Operations
  and Rural Development Supports)
  64, 136
MACV (Military Assistance Com-
  mand, Vietnam) *45*
Mai *21, 36*
Major *238*
Malaysia *173, 203, 204, 221, 222*
Mandarin (Chinese) *204*
Marine *144, 145, 146*
Marvin *180, 184, 202, 218, 219, 227*
Marx, Carl *23*
Massachusetts *240*
McGriffert, John R. ,Brig. Gen. *120*
Mekong Delta *221, 230*
MIA (Missing in action) *123*
Military Advisory Team *47 see Index A*
Miller, William H., Col. *71*
Mine Alley *41, 242*
Ministry of Foreign Affairs *173*
Mo Tran, To (Joyce) *167*
MR3 (Military Region III) *71, 121, 122*
Murphy *59*
Muslim *211*
My Chanh Hamlet *55*
My Lai *56*
My Tho *221*

N

Nam Son Square *146*
National Leadership Committee *33*
NCO (Non-commission Officer) *59*
New International Version (Bible) *216*
New Year *44, 46*
New Zealand *227*
NLF (National Liberation Front) *30,*
  149, 230, 231
Ngo Dinh Luyen *30*
Ngo Dinh Can *30*
Ngo Dinh Diem *26, 29, 30, 31, 33*
Ngo Dinh Nhu *30*
Ngo Dinh Thuc *30*
Ngo Quyen Street *145*
Nguyen Can Hai *156, 157, 158, 159*
Nguyen Chan A *146, 147, 151, 152*
Nguyen Cong Son *136, 137*
Nguyen Cong Thanh, Col. *141*
Nguyen Cong Vinh, Col. *70, 78*
Nguyen Hue Easter Offensive *128*
Nguyen Hue Street *146*
Nguyen Huu Co, Maj. Gen. *153*
Nguyen Thien Thuat *147*
Nguyen Van Hieu, Brig. Gen. *121*
Nguyen Van Nam *230*
Nguyen Van Thanh *57*
Nguyen Van Thieu *33, 45, 133, 143*
Nguyen Van Thinh, Major *74, 76, 78,*
  79, 80
Nguyen Van Tuong *72, 82*
Ninh thanh Hamlet *99*
Nixon, Richard *141*
Nolde, William B., Lt. Col *134*

North Vietnam(ese) *25, 26, 30, 31, 33, 34, 133, 148, 151, 152,155, 163, 169, 224, 230, 244*
NVA (North Vietnamese Army) *30, 39, 44, 46, 47, 50, 58, 60, 65, 66, 67, 71, 72, 74, 75, 76, 78, 79, 80, 81, 82, 85, 86, 87, 92, 96, 99, 103, 105, 111, 113, 115, 125, 127128, 129, 130, 134, 143, 145, 147 150, 155, 156, 163, 164, 172, 186, 230*

O

ODP (Orderly Departure Program) *236*
Operation Linebacker II *133*

P

Paris Peace Treaty *133, 155, 163*
Pastor *141*
Peace Treaty *141*
People's Tribunal *163, 169*
PF (Popular Force) *43, 47, 48, 53, 60*
Pham Quang My *66, 75*
Phan Thiet *175*
Phat *182, 185, 188, 192, 207*
Philippine *222*
Phnom Penh *166*
Phu Cuong *129, 133, 134, 137, 141*
Phu Loi *35*
Phuc Kien High School *22*
Phung Hung Street *22*
Phuoc Long Province *141*
Pier *73 192, 194*
PK3399 Boat *179, 182, 183, 184, 187 192, 210, 215, 223, 235*
Political Warfare School *143, 145*
POW (Prisoner of War) *84*

Precinct *185, 186, 187, 188*
Province Chief *63, 114*
Province Senior Advisor *6*
Psalm *16, 102*
Psychological Warfare Headquarters *147*
PT76 Soviet-made tank *126, 134*
Purge and Property Inventory Campaign *169, 182, 231*
Purple Heart Medal *121*

Q

QL-13 (National Highway) *40, 41, 42, 50, 57, 66, 75, 95, 106, 107, 109, 111, 126, 130, 242*
Quan Loi *40, 75*
Quang Tri *143*
Quang Zhou Province *17*
Quang, Lt. *76, 79*

R

R & R (Rest and Recuperation) *70, 139*
Reconnaissance Company *49*
Red Cross *169*
Republic of China (Taiwan) *146, 148*
Republic of Vietnam *156*
RF (Regional Force) *43, 47, 48, 57, 70, 72, 77, 79, 95, 126, 137*
Riau Archipelago *228*
Riau Islands Province *209*
Rice, Robert *125*
Rogers, William *133*
Rome Plow Team *41*
RPG-40 rocket launcher *66, 85, 102*
Rung Sat Swamp *30*

Tran Tan Phuoc, 2nd Lt. *114, 115, 117, 118*
Tran Van Huong *143*
Tran Van Nhut, Col. *63, 119, 141*
Tran Van Tan *60*
Treasury Department (South Vietnam) *143*
Treaty of Friendship of Cooperation *176*
Tri (Marvin) *180*

U

United Kingdom *30*
UN (United Nations) *227, 228, 229*
UNHCR (United Nations High Commissioner for Refugees) *211, 212, 216, 219, 222, 228, 236*
United States of America *23, 25, 31, 70, 227, 229, 232, 233, 236, 238*
U.S. Army Corps of Engineers *41, 42, 64, 66*
U.S. Congress *34, 155*
U.S. Defense Attaché's Office *144*
U.S. Embassy *144, 146*
U.S. Government *155*
U.S. Military Advisor *126*
U.S. Special Force *42*
U.S.S. Maddox *34*
U.S.S. Turner *34*
Uu Long Street *19*

V

Vacation Bible School *191*

VC (Viet Cong) *26, 30, 33, 34, 41, 44, 45, 46, 48, 50, 55, 57, 59, 60, 65, 67, 72, 83, 84, 98, 109, 113, 148, 149, 166, 224, 225, 230, 236*
Viet Cong Provisional Revolutionary Government *148*
Viet Minh *25, 26, 27, 28, 30, 157*
Vietnam *17, 21, 25, 26, 31, 33, 34, 35, 41, 51, 57, 67, 174, 176, 222, 224, 235, 236, 238, 241*
Vietnam War *33, 34, 44, 47, 149, 175, 222, 236, 242*
Vietnam War Veterans *236*
Vietnamese *209, 216, 224, 228*
Vietnamese Labor Party *230, 231*
Vung Tau *139, 142, 175, 179, 194*

W

Wallingford, Kenneth, Sgt. *119*
Wanat Jr., George K., Capt. *70, 73, 74, 79, 80, 83, 84, 85, 86, 95, 97, 119, 130, 237, 240, 241*
War Zone C *xi, 39*
War Zone D *39*
Washington D.C. *31, 155*
Waterford, Connecticut *70*
Whampoa Military Academy *147*
World Vision *216*
WWII *25, 27, 74, 147*

X

XM134 Vulcan mini gun *97*
Xom Cui *28*

Y

Yearta, Jesse SFC *127*
Yellow Bullies *19*

32555425R00145

Made in the USA
Lexington, KY
24 May 2014